IMPACT OF HISTORY ON THEOLOGY
Thoughts of a Czech Pastor

Josef L. Hromadka

IMPACT OF HISTORY
ON THEOLOGY
Thoughts of a Czech Pastor

FIDES PUBLISHERS, INC.
Notre Dame, Indiana

Translated from the Czech by Monika and Benjamin Page
Published originally in French by Les Éditions du Cerf
under the title *Pour Quoi Je Vis*

© Copyright: 1970, Fides Publishers, Inc.
Notre Dame, Indiana
Library of Congress Catalog Card Number: 78-108029
Standard Book Number: 8190-0521-5

Printed in Great Britain

CONTENTS

I FROM RESTLESSNESS OF SPIRIT TO THEOLOGY   I
The years before 1914
  The First Serious Questions   3
  Schools and Teachers   9

II WAR, REVOLUTION AND A FEEBLE PEACE   22
1914–34
  War and Revolution   22
  Catholicism and the Struggle for Christianity   40
  The Orthodox Church and the Soviets   45
  Europe's Crisis: A Test of Theology   50
  A Diagnosis of German Protestantism   52

III AMERICAN VICTORY IN THE YEARS OF CHAOS   58
1939–47
  American Theological and Political Dilemmas   58
  The Second World War   65
  Secularization: Opportunity and Threat for
    Mankind   68

IV ON THE RUINS OF THE SECOND WORLD WAR   72
  Account of my Stay in America   72
  Czechoslovakia after the War   75
  The Danger of a Ghetto   80
  Questions about Atheism   82
  History does not stand still either for Christians or
    for Communists   85
  Questions of the Dialogue: What is Man?   92
  What is Sacred for Man?   93

The Christian Peace Conference   98
History, Faith, Politics   103
The Crossroads of Socialism   105
The Dynamics of the Foundations   111
The Consolation of Theology   113

Bibliography of the most important works of
  Josef Hromadka   116

ONE

From Restlessness of Spirit
to Theology

The Years before 1914

The Slav consciousness

It might help in understanding my activities in theology and the Church if we begin with the area where I was born and grew up. My native village is in the north-eastern part of Moravia, on the border between Moravian Wallachia and Kravaria (Lassko). The headlands of the Beskyd mountains give the region a special charm. The boundary between Moravia and Silesia is not far off.

My village is in a region where the people already speak with a slight Polish accent. Everything about the manner and appearance of the people of Lassko differentiates them from the Moravian Wallachians. Despite this, a deep spiritual tradition has closely bound our Protestants to the villages of Wallachia, for there was a rather large number of them still holding out secretly in the mountains. Their presence was due partly to the fact that it was very difficult to penetrate the nooks and crannies of the mountains, so that the influence of the Counter-Reformation was very restricted, and partly to the proximity of the city of Tesin, where, in 1709, Protestants were allowed to build their so-called Church of Grace (*Gnaden-kirche*).

Pietistic influences from Tesin had a perceptible effect on

our village, strongly colouring the atmosphere of the secret Protestant groups from the end of the seventeenth century until 1781, when the Edict of Tolerance was issued. The Church in Tesin attracted these Protestants and sustained their spiritual lives. It is worth mentioning that it was from our region that Christian David went to Saxony and, together with Count Zinzendorf, founded the Community of Herrnhut (*Bruder-gemeinde*). Several Protestant families followed him, which is the reason for the name 'Moravian Brothers' (Moravians), by which these Herrnhut Christians are known in the Anglo-Saxon world. It can thus be said that the Protestant communities which developed in this eastern part of Moravia are in a very real way related to the classical period of the Czech Reformation, from the time of Jan Hus (executed in 1415) until the battle of White Mountain (1620).

The people of my native region are as close geographically to Poland as they are to Slovakia. The change to a Polish landscape begins in my village, and it was a long time before a definite border line between Polish and Czech ethnic characteristics existed in the consciousness of the people of the Tesin area of Silesia. The transition between languages is gradual, and it is impossible to determine precisely where Czech ends and Polish begins. Of course the culture of us Moravians has for centuries been organically related to that of the Czechs, but the frontiers in Tesin (Silesia) were established on a permanent basis only in the last century.

I might mention in passing that the great seventeenth-century Protestant hymn-writer, Jiri Tranovsky, belongs to all three peoples, the Czechs, the Poles, and the Slovaks. He lived at a time when the inhabitants of this region were united, despite all language differences; it was only gradually that they became separate from each other.

Perhaps it is only how it seems to me in retrospect, but when I look back over my childhood, I have the impression that my way of thinking was more Slav than Czech. Poles, Slovaks, and Czechs, all are fused in me into a single whole.

The First Serious Questions

The glory of Palacky

This should in no way suggest, of course, that we were not aware of our part in the vital traditions of Czech history. Our Protestant community was Lutheran, but the consciousness that we were anchored in the *Czech* Reformation and that our first great Reform leader was Jan Hus, was at the heart of our spiritual make-up. Our village was very proud of the fact that it was the birthplace of Frantisek Palacky, leader of the Czech national revival and one of our greatest historians and political leaders of the nineteenth century. His father, a teacher in the church school of the congregation which had been permitted to have its organizations under the Edict of Toleration, instilled in him a respect and a love for the tradition of the Czech Reformation. He was responsible for the building of the Protestant church school at which I eventually studied. The fame of Palacky infected our entire village, awakening in us a vivid awareness of Czech history.

Frantisek Palacky was destined by his father to become a pastor in the church which emerged from the Edict of Toleration. As a young student he once preached in our church about 'true Christian piety'. But his interest in literature, and his love of poetry and particularly of the history of his nation diverted him from his theological studies and directed him, via Trenchin and the lyceum at Pressburg (Bratislava), towards Prague, where he was to work unstintingly. In our family we often

3

remembered the tragic struggles of the Czech Reformation, and began to develop a deep interest in history.

Czech patriotism

Another important point, however, must be mentioned in this connection. My native village, Hodslavice, lies right on an ethnic frontier. The next town was already German and the chief town of our district, Novy Jicin, was one of those towns where a large part of the population was under the influence of pan-German ideas and had an antipathy for anything Czech. Even when our country was still under Austria there was a popular saying that ten Viennese plus another one were not equal to one man from Novy Jicin. This aggressive nationalism on the part of the Germans aroused among their Czech neighbours very strong feelings of patriotism. Today when I look back on the time of my youth, I cannot help asking whether we Moravian Czechs were not perhaps even more loyal to Old Austria than were its pan-German citizens, who wanted to win over Austria for the interests of the Germans, yes, for the German Empire and the Hohenzollerns.

While still in my youth I began to change from thinking like a Slav to thinking in terms of being a Czech. It was as a result of these pan-German ambitions that I gradually became more and more anti-Austrian. As far as I can see the real grave-diggers of the Austro-Hungarian Empire were the Germans rather than any of the Slavic peoples.

Frantisek Palacky, as a Czech statesman and politician, sought to save the Austrian Empire from these pan-German ambitions. It was only towards the end of his life that he began to grow sceptical and to wonder whether Austria could be saved from the storms that were taking shape around German expansionism. Palacky derived much from the rich cultural traditions of German idealism—in particular Kant and Herder—but he also embodied a kind of synthesis of the legacies of the Czech Reformation of the fifteenth to seventeeth centuries and the whole of Czech historical tradition from the time of St Wenceslaus in the tenth century. Even though he interpreted the meaning of Czech history as a constant feud between Czechs and Germans, he did not think of Czech history in anti-German terms. Rather, he sought to show that from the outset the struggle, both critical and positive, with German culture has been part of Czech history.

During my youth the good relations between the Czech and German inhabitants of our villages began to break down. The character of these relations became increasingly strained and by the time of the first world war there were few Czechs, even among us in Moravia, whose hearts were on the side of the Austro-Hungarian Empire. It was then already clear that a victory for Germany and Austria would have meant a drastic weakening, if not crippling, of the Slavic peoples squeezed in between the two central European powers.

Amidst progressive influences

I come of peasant stock. My father was one of the most respected peasants in the village. My life was thus closely bound up with that of the rural peasant. But even during my student years I was deeply interested in what was at that time the birth of the labour movement. Many of my co-citizens in the village worked in industry or at the tobacco factory in the chief town, where they came into contact with socialist ideas, propagated primarily by the Social Democratic Party. From the first our national struggles were related to social consciousness. But by the beginning of this century, in Czech-speaking regions as elsewhere, a split began to develop between these two currents. Thus, for example, next door to the local headquarters of Sokol, a nationalist athletic organization, stood the social-democratic trade union building. Through my family I tended to identify with Sokol's nationalism, but at the same time I was a strong supporter of the social and socialist struggles of our working class. This was probably the result of the influence of three of our most prominent figures, T. G. Masaryk, and Frant. Drtina, professors at the University of Prague, and the fiery poet J. S. Machar who, at the turn of the century, became involved, even as a poet and critic of Czech and Austrian life, in our literary and even our political struggles.

Czech Protestantism was influenced by Masaryk because he had left the Roman Catholic Church to become a member of the reformed evangelical church, and because he took over from Palacky his view of Czech history, especially his high esteem for the Reformation of Hus and the Unity of Brethren. Masaryk often said that the Czech question was a religious question, that our national revival was a continuation of the Czech Reformation, and that our national and political programme should be inspired by the humanism of the reformation era, that is, by the struggle for freedom, justice and social progress. These views corresponded, at the time, with the hopes and efforts of Czech Protestants. Czech Protestantism, at the turn of the century, was still bound up with the countryside. It can be said without exaggeration that the Protestantism of that time—before the arrival of socialist parties on the scene—was one of the most progressive currents in Czech life. All of these reasons explain how it was possible for Masaryk and his colleagues to have such a great influence on the spiritual life of Protestantism. They are also what led me to my active interest in social questions and social democracy. Although I

6

have never taken part in direct political activity nor joined a political party, my interest in politics in the deeper meaning of the word, as well as in social questions, has been very great since my student days.

The thirst for knowledge

However, in my case this interest was outweighed by an even greater interest in literature, especially poetry and history. Closely related was an openness towards all spiritual and religious ferment. The last decade of the nineteenth century was characterized, in the Czech area of the old Hapsburg Empire, by turbulent intellectual, literary, and political activity; it was as if all the currents of the world had come together on the soil of our national life. The birth and revival of our people, which began at the end of the eighteenth century, began to bear fruit, after many a struggle, towards the end of the 1870s. In the 'eighties our first scientists began to challenge the old myths. For example, scientific methods were used to demonstrate the falsity of the so-called manuscripts of Dvur Kralove and Zelena Hora. Then, during the 'nineties, all the schools of literature, philosophy, culture, and politics converged on us at once. Tolstoi with his anarchism, Dostoevsky with his pitiless pyschological analysis of the depths of the human spirit, French decadence, the national messianisms in which romantic storms and dreams were enacted, revolts against church tradition and against religious certainties and illusions, Nietzsche with his Zarathustrian superman 'beyond good and evil', Catholic modernism coloured by superficial sentimentalism and, alongside all this, the realism of Masaryk with its efforts to found our national life on the firm foundations of Reformation humanism and positive religion.

All of this was going on at the time I was finishing secondary

7

school (*gymnasium*) and trying to decide which university discipline would offer me the best opportunity of satisfying both my scientific and my spiritual aspirations. For a few months I inclined towards the study of Czech literature, history and, of course, philosophy, in which I was influenced by our foremost philosophers. In addition to Masaryk these included Drtina and F. Krejci, not only because of their academic activity but also because of their energetic efforts to raise the cultural and moral levels of Czech life.

Getting to the roots

When I look back on my last two years in secondary school, I am astonished at how I was able to decide so suddenly and almost unconditionally in favour of theology. I relate this decision to the influence of my slightly older friend, Theodore Kalenda. Kalenda had finished studying Protestant theology in Vienna and Bonn, and before going abroad he visited me in Valasske Mezirici. We discussed our spiritual problems and life plans. I complained to him that I could not adhere to any of the contemporary intellectual or spiritual schools of thought. It seemed to me that I was not sufficiently anchored in the traditional life of the church to be able to control the storms and confusion of my uneasy young heart. It was not negation or nihilism that threatened the interior state of my life; it was simply confusion and uncertainty. The stormy revolt against religion and the Church at that time was directed especially against official clerical Catholicism with its close ties with the Hapsburg dynasty. Even so, however, something of the spark of this struggle penetrated even among us young Protestant intellectuals. We were saved from negation by a sentimental attachment to our minority church, its difficult history, its considerable standard of thinking and its progressive outlook.

8

Even so, however, Tolstoi and Nietzsche, with his slogan, 'God is dead', the action of 'free thought', J. S. Machar and the advent of socialism, which at that time still bore traces of positivism, could not fail to affect us young students with our passion for literature and our immersion in the cultural influences of the time. I repeat, it was a time when the best spokesmen for our nation were battering at the boundaries of our provincialism and self-satisfaction. Doors and windows opened wide. It was no longer a question of the existence of the nation, as had been the case one hundred years before at the time of the national rebirth. It was a question of broadening our spiritual horizons in all directions, and of taking part as equals with the people of other nations on the stage of Europe.

All of this was the subject of our youthful—often naïve, but still sincere—debates. When I laid my troubles, uncertainties, and hopes before my friend Kalenda, he asked simply: Why not study theology and thus get at the roots of the questions of life and hope? That simple question decided the future course of my studies. I abandoned thoughts of studying Czech literature and history and decided to go into theology. Before I actually began studying, theology had seemed to me to be a philosophy of religion, rather than the theology of the Bible and the Church.

SCHOOLS AND TEACHERS

In the last analysis . . .

The road to theology led me to Vienna, in the autumn of 1907; at that time Czech Protestants had no theological schools of their own. All Protestants of the Austrian Empire—Czechs, Germans, Poles and the rest—were required to study at least some of their theology courses at the school in Vienna, where we also had to be examined by the highest ecclesiastical authorities. So it was that I entered on the normal activity of a central European school of theology.

At first I had to satisfy my interest in religious philosophy with more or less private studies and occasional visits to the philosophy lectures at the University of Vienna. The chairman of the department there was Friedrich Jodl, a Feuerbach-style positivist. Although a committed fighter for a religionless morality, he also had a serious understanding of the problems of modern man. I very much enjoyed listening to him, but I had a strong feeling that his view of the storms and abysses of the time did not equal Masaryk's analysis of the contemporary religious crisis. 'Suicide', Masaryk's study of this crisis in the works of Kant, Goethe, Hume, Musset, Byron, Dostoevsky, and other modern European writers, prepared me much better for what, in the last analysis, is the ultimate reality of the biblical message and the creative force in church history.

Of my theology professors, I remember with gratitude Rudolph Knopf, a young New Testament specialist, for his discussions on apostolic and post-apostolic times. I am also indebted to Ernst Sellin, an Old Testament scholar and biblical archaeologist, who unfortunately left the school in Vienna before we could get very deep into his interpretations of the Old Testament.

A necessary road

I was soon quite caught up in biblical theology, and for some years thought of specializing in the New Testament. I was influenced in this direction by teachers in Vienna, and also at the University of Basel. The most influential of these were Paul Wernle and, a little later, in Heidelberg, Johannes Weiss. This was the period of the so-called synoptical questions, and the 'history of religions' school. Such names as W. Wrede, W. Bousset and Adolf Jülicher were in the forefront of discussion about the New Testament, along with those I have already named. For a long time the figure of St Paul was, if not foreign, at least very distant from my more intensive biblical interests. I agreed with those who saw a deep difference between Jesus and Paul; so, for a long time it was impossible for me to get down to the roots of faith in the ultimate meaning of the Gospel revelation of the descent of the God of Israel to the depths of human weakness, sin and despair. But then, this may have been a necessary road for a young student vacillating between scepticism and certainty, between authority and freedom, and who sought a secular interpretation of religious history and of what we call Revelation. But even on the level of what was then modern biblical theology, I began to understand, both theoretically and practically, that neither history nor psychology was sufficient for understanding what happened when God called Abraham and Moses, Elijah, Amos, Jeremiah and the other prophets to become his witnesses, or when the apostles came to believe in Jesus as Christ.

I remember the interpretations of the prophets and the psalms by my Old Testament teacher, B. Duhm, at Basel. After all his penetrating literary and historical analyses of the biblical texts, in which he often divided the old documents into several historical groups, he never failed to remind us, his index finger raised, that the life commitments of biblical witnesses were the result of the intervention into their own lives from above, that what was involved was a mystery which it is impossible to interpret or explain to human thought by scientific-humanist methods.

And with the same clarity I recall those moments when, in a seminar on church history, we were analysing St Augustine's efforts to preserve the irreducible revelation in the midst of the Hellenistic-Roman civilization. In the midst of reading Harnack's discussion on Augustine in his *Dogmengeschichte* I was suddenly shattered by the insight into the abyss of human sinfulness and impotence. I should mention that my increasing existential—and I do not mean existentialist!—understanding of biblical history from Abraham through Paul was in no way a flight from science, criticism, or from literary and historical analysis of the books of the Bible or the dogmatic formulae of the early Christians. In the period of my most radically critical thinking in theology, I had already become aware of the fact that theology is not based on human experience, on the laws of spiritual life, or of evolution and historical progress; on the contrary, what theology deals with are those realities that are beyond human categories and methods.

A potent fermentation

But there is one more stage of my theological struggles that must be mentioned. After my studies and final exams in 1911 I left for the University of Heidelberg. There I was attracted by three people: first by Ernst Troeltsch, already a well-known representative of the so-called *Religionsgeschichtliche Schule*. He, perhaps more systematically than anyone else, expressed the main tendencies of modern theology in the early part of the twentieth century. For him, Christianity was losing itself in the historical and psychical evolution of mankind—beyond the limits not only of Christian but of other religious groupings as well. He took the laws of historical and social evolution so seriously that the problem of truth and its criteria became for him a very difficult subject, one involving a deep spiritual struggle. The truth and realism of his views of history and society, hence also of the development of the Church, captivated his audiences and introduced a potent fermentation into contemporary theology.

I studied under him just at the time when he was completing his classic work on *The Social Teaching of the Christian Churches*. For him the conflict between Christian motives and all aspects of cultural life (in social relations, in government and law, in the family and in individual morality) was the object of penetrating study, which came to serve as a healthy antidote to the purely dogmatic, liturgical, and pastoral content of normal theology. Troeltsch's work became the target of much criticism; church and theological circles took especially sharp issue with his analysis of the Church of the Lutheran conception (Karl Holl's book on Luther being but one of many examples I could mention). Even so, however, he helped us young theologians to look at the history of the Church from a new vantage point, and to understand the problems of modern Christianity in the light of the social and political upheavals of the time.

After the first world war, Ernst Troeltsch came out in support of the Weimar Republic and decried the narrow limits of German Lutheranism as unhappily bound up with the currents of restoration that could be found in the German churches of the early post-war period. His analysis of West European and Anglo-Saxon ecclesiastical forms opened up to him a broad political view and an awareness of those aspects of German tradition and nationalism which represented danger not only for the German people, but for the people of Europe and the rest of the civilized world as well. Even as one of his students before the first world war I could sense something of the breadth of his scope. And it is this breadth that places him vastly above the average among university professors of the time.

The dilemma

Of course even at that time I had thought a great deal about the weaknesses of his theology. I had become aware, although perhaps not with complete precision, that his theology was in fact more a philosophy of religion, that he was unable fully to discern the core of the Christian faith and biblical message. He often repeated that Christianity is concerned with a particular idea, in contrast to the ideological constructions of antiquity, of Greek or Roman culture, and of course in contrast also with non-Christian religions. There was a singular, but explicable, contradiction between his historicism and his reduction of Christian faith to the level of a mere ideological aspect of spiritual life. All that takes place between God and man was lost, for him, in the inner spiritual pressure of human existence. He sought to preserve what we call religion, referring to a religious *a priori*; that is to say, the pressure within man which is inescapable and which could not be explained by interior faith or by the structure of the human mind. Just as we talk about the *a priori* nature of the category of reason, or of moral and aesthetic norms, we can also talk about the *a priori* nature of man's relationships with the absolute foundations of life and being. Troeltsch himself later revised his thesis, but in essence he was never able to grasp that which forms the central nerve and core of the message of the Old and New Testaments; he never managed to get beyond the limits of his own historical relativism. Christianity appeared to him as but one form of religion. This is what gave him the right to question Christianity's claim to being absolute.

It is true that Christianity as a historical form is subject to the facts of historical relativity. But this form is created and constantly recreated by reality and by forces that go beyond the process of history, forces that can be understood only in the context of history, but which even so transcend historical necessity. We can use the word 'revelation' for this reality and these forces, but we must bear in mind that no concept can express the real depth and dynamism of what is involved. But Troeltsch, despite his extraordinary historical preceptiveness, never grasped the core of faith and personal decision. That is why even in his book, *The Social Teaching of the Christian Churches*, he let himself be too much influenced by the idea of natural law as the basic motive in the social and political consequences of faith, failing to comprehend the actual motive force of the biblical message about creation, about the Word as a creative force, about the incarnation, crucifixion, and resurrection of Christ.

Troeltsch, of course, was so penetrating an observer of religious life that he was able to understand the significance of the liturgy in the religious community. He saw that not even the Christian Church made sense without the liturgical relationship of the believer to Jesus Christ, without the invocation of his being, or without prayer to him. But he saw in this reality only psychological and sociological necessity. By this he did not mean the psychological and sociological necessity of the descent of the supreme God to the level of human life, poverty, and frailty; what he meant was the necessity of the cult as the centre around which to create a community.

It was on this point that I began my critical re-examination of Troeltsch's theological thought. I did not turn my back on the problems he raised, but rather struggled critically with him at the point where he left off in his theological interpretations and seemed almost to sense himself in a dead end. I later began to feel that Troeltsch had terminated his theological crusade at the next-to-the-last station, if not before. This is how he came to end his working life not as a theologian, but as a professor of philosophy, at the University of Berlin.

These criticisms are in no way intended as a denial of Troeltsch's greatness as a thinker and later—after 1918—as a political observer and even as a statesman. Even though my roots are Czech and my outlook was shaped by Czech problems and cultural influences, I had the strong impression that Troeltsch was one of those who could have done something about the condition of the spiritual life of the German churches, who might have been able to stem the tide of restoration and nationalism within German Protestantism after the first world war.

I may be running ahead of historical continuity, but I often ask myself and my present colleagues, from a contemporary perspective, whether the whole development of German theology, including its rediscovery of Luther, did not perhaps take a wrong turn for the same reason that Ernst Troeltsch was neglected, and whether several of the ideas of his theological and cultural thought were not, perhaps by his own fault, prematurely side-tracked.

Other Heidelberg teachers I cannot forget are Johannes Weiss and Wilhelm Windelband, the one a New Testament scholar and the other a philosopher. Weiss introduced me to the serious study of the New Testament and Windelband to the questions relating to the frontiers between theology and philosophy. Even so, however, work in Troeltsch's seminars and his expositions of ethics and comparative study of Christian churches so outweighed all other influences that, in my theological work, I have stayed in the field of systematics. It never occurred to me, during my student years, that I might become a professor. I saw before me, despite certain spiritual vacillations, a career as a preacher, but my interest, despite my love of New Testament studies, became increasingly centred on questions of systematics and dogmatics.

I experience the Church

After my second theological examination, which was required before one could begin pastoral activity, I set out, in the autumn of 1911, for Scotland, in order to learn about the theological and ecclesiastical life of that country. Scotland was particularly important to me as a Czech because our Reformed Church communities maintained close relations with the United Free Church of Scotland. Although I was a Lutheran theologian, I was drawn towards the Presbyterian milieu. The months I spent at the college of the United Free Church in Aberdeen were unexpectedly profitable and important for me. I clearly felt the Church as the very ground beneath my feet. There were still traces in the United Free Church of the spiritual revival movement which had led to the Disruption of the Church of Scotland in 1843—which was, in fact, the principal cause of it and of other spiritual influences within the church, especially that of the development of Protestant Scottish missions.

What particularly impressed me were the close ties between theological studies and the church. Having come from the academic situation of central European theology, the atmosphere in the Scottish theological college was something quite new for me. From the outset I was puzzled both by the small size of the college and by the level of theological activity. My theological outlook was enriched by the growing conviction that real theology, while still critical and scientific, must grow out of the living fellowship of the Church. Theology cannot be real if it is not anchored in the Church of the apostles and in the community of the people of the Old Testament. Moreover, we cannot understand by piety or by scientific methods

17

the documents of the Bible, the struggle to grasp the ultimate truths of faith, or even the creative intervention of the Church in the cultural lives of nations, unless we experience our theological problems among people who listen to the Word of God, who assemble for hymns and prayers, and who are conscious of the mission given to them by the God of history himself, who was present in him who was crucified and rose from the dead—a fellowship constantly transformed by the living God of truth and grace.

As I look back on my theological development, I can say that I have never forsaken what I learned at previous theological faculties. I have never looked down on the critical and scientific theology which penetrates so disquietingly into the life of the Church. But on a deeper level I thought a great deal about the genuine message of the Bible. I was not completely unprepared. I have already mentioned Bernard Duhm and his exposition of the Old Testament. Even so, it seemed to me that I had not yet fully understood the heart of the Gospel itself and that several articles of the early Christian confession of faith were still foreign to me. I did not fully understand that each account by an apostle or by a prophet expresses not just an idea or a thought, but more than anything else, an action, an actual intervention from above, which lies outside and beyond all human concepts and categories. Not even in Scotland did I get to the essence of theology, but I did come to understand and experience much more than previously the mystery of the almighty God of love and grace. Above all, I was caught up in the stream of church community life.

A world-wide perspective

There are two teachers whom I particularly remember, James Stalker, a church historian, and David S. Cairns, a systematic theologian. At the time, Cairns' name was on the lips of every Scottish student and churchman. The year before my arrival, there had taken place in Edinburgh the first missionary conference (1910) which is considered today to have marked the beginning of the present ecumenical movement and even of the World Council of Churches. The principal organizer of the conference was John R. Mott, a missionary strategist and a statesman, and one of the founders of the World Student Christian Federation.

David S. Cairns was an excellent speaker; he found living words to formulate the aims of the conference. In him, the passion of faith was united with missionary fervour and a broad understanding of inter-church community. He was a man who had studied modern theological thought, but who remained firmly rooted in the traditions of the Scottish Reformation. He lived in the fullness of the biblical message in the form which it had taken in Scotland, through struggle and suffering, during the course of fierce contest with the Roman Catholic Church, the established Episcopal Church, and finally with the atmosphere of the rationalism and erastianism of a state church which had yielded to the secularism of the Enlightenment.

If I was dissatisfied, at first, with the lack of the kind of academic atmosphere to which I had become accustomed in the other schools where I had studied, I acquired a broad view of Anglo-Saxon Protestantism, of the cosmopolitanism of British political thought, and especially of the missionary zeal of the ordinary member of the Scottish Church. I came to see how our central European theological and ecclesiastical life bore the marks of a certain provincialism, and how narrow-minded German national self-consciousness appeared in comparison with the world outlook of Scottish Protestantism and with British Protestantism, in general.

But at the same time, I felt an inner anguish at the sight of the vast differences between the conventional, well-fed, and contented churchmen, on the one side, and the indescribable poverty of the poorer classes who lived in the slums of every larger city. During my stay in Scotland the social question took on a much more urgent character than it ever had for me in the countries of central Europe. David Cairns certainly also had in the fervent core of his faith a fine sense for the social poverty of the so-called lowest classes, and in his theological lectures he was able to show how the Gospel brings help to the poor and to the most miserable. Even the miracles of the Bible lost, for him, their miraculous character. He rejected the idea that the miracles were subsequent additions attempting to prove the divinity and authority of Jesus Christ. He saw the acts and miracles of Jesus as expressions of his boundless love and his compassionate descent towards those who were suffering in spirit or body. Jesus actually helped to deliver people from blindness and deafness, from leprosy, hunger, and bodily poverty in general. D. S. Cairns was not among the foremost of contemporary theologians. However, he was an extraordinary personality, as profound as he was generous in his burning hope that the Kingdom of God has been moving forward from the times of the Old Covenant and that in Jesus of Nazareth it is in the midst of us. Loyalty to his own church was in him united with an ardent understanding for other churches, for the sufferings of modern man, and for our obligations towards the people of non-Christian countries.

The world in which I lived during my stay in Aberdeen no longer exists. The British Empire, which nurtured in its citizens the pride of being citizens of the world, was weakened by the first world war and ceased to exist soon after 1945. With the Empire died also the hope, so impressively expressed by John R. Mott and D. S. Cairns, that the Gospel would be spread to the entire world in their own generation. Something else also passed from the scene in the wake of the second world war: the conviction that Western, so-called Christian civilization would be a model for the whole world, that an international order would gradually develop in the direction of Western culture with its Christian norms, with the support of British wisdom and American wealth and free enterprise.

Be that as it may, I am sincerely indebted to these men for the deepening of my theological thinking and of my spiritual life, for having made me aware of the missionary responsibility of the living Church, and for introducing me to a world-wide perspective as I have experienced it under the leadership of D. S. Cairns and in the Student Christian Movement.

TWO

War, Revolution and a
Feeble Peace

1914–1934

IN THE SPRING OF 1912 I returned home, via Paris. At the time, of course, I was hardly aware that the twilight of the old Europe had begun to fall, that we were then standing on the demarcation line between two epochs. (I was en route from Paris to Germany when the *Titanic* sank.) We were all conscious of the tension between France and Germany, and events in the Balkans were deepening the dispute between Austro-Hungary and Tsarist Russia. But we were so used to peace that we could not even imagine the possibility of a bloody conflict among the European powers.

WAR AND REVOLUTION

A disturbing conclusion

That summer I began my pastoral activity in a Lutheran congregation in Vsetin in Eastern Moravia. In this region, there was then a larger percentage of Protestants—both Lutherans and Reformed—than anywhere in the Czech region. I was ordained on September 8, 1912, by a representative of the Moravo-Silesian district, the Polish Lutheran, Superintendent Glajcar. I devoted myself to my work with a real inner passion. Fortunately I had my Scottish experience behind me, so that the results of my studies in Central European faculties were already integrated into an awareness of the mission of the Church and of the message of the Bible and the Reformation.

But I remember how it took me several years to develop my theological thinking into an internally coherent whole. I do not know how my sermons might have benefited a Wallachian Protestant, but I put everything I then had, spiritually, into my religious instruction in the schools and into my work with young people. I was thus able to test the capacities of the various theological trends, which brought me to the rather disquieting conclusion that so-called modern theology did not have much of that strength of which churches are built; the work of the supposedly conservative pastors was, at the time, showing itself to be far more fruitful and creative.

The Reformed congregations of Moravia were served by a group of preachers which had grown up under the influence of Hermann Kohlbrugge and his son-in-law, Eduard Bohl, a professor at the Theological Faculty in Vienna. As an assistant minister of a Lutheran congregation I had the growing impression that the Reformed congregations were much more alive, both ecclesiastically and theologically, and that the unification of the two would benefit both. We sought to break down confessional barriers among the young people, and to create an atmosphere of genuine co-operation—with only occasional success. The division among Czech Protestants seemed to me ever more anachronistic; moreover it absorbed much of the energy we could have been devoting to work in public life.

The unfinished revolution

International tensions mounted; the Balkan wars of 1912-13 augured ill. Yet we were still sure that Europe's crises would be overcome; the idea of a large-scale war was, at the beginning of the twentieth century, unthinkable. Even the death of the heir to the Austro-Hungarian throne, Archduke Franz Ferdinand, seemed at first no more than a warning to the statesmen of Europe. But a month later—August 1914—the first world war broke out, and shattered the old world irreparably.

The Czech people as a whole, especially we Protestants, took the side of those countries fighting against the so-called Central Powers, Kaiser Germany and the Austro-Hungarian Empire. This was particularly true because our action of opposition was led from abroad by T. G. Masaryk, in whom we had unbounded faith. Of course none of us had any idea what kind of Europe would emerge from the breaking up of the Empire and the defeat of the powerful military strength of the German Reich. We were quite unprepared, from the viewpoints both of theology and of the philosophy of history, for a war of such fearful dimensions; even less could we know that we were then standing on the threshold of a revolution of world-wide dimensions that has not yet come to an end. All we could see was that changes were taking place in the context of international politics. We believed that the victory of the anti-German allies would bring greater democracy to our country and free those peoples hitherto subject to the Central European powers. Everywhere the Social Democratic Parties supported their national governments; reinforcing our feeling that what was most needed was changes in the area of political democracy and national self-determination. But what was then shaken was the very structure of European civilization as it had developed from the Middle Ages up through to its contemporary socio-political forms.

After 1917

The revolutionary year of 1917 enabled us to see better and more profoundly the roots and structure of European culture. By that time I had already arrived in Prague as pastor to the congregation at the Salvator church. Initially we sympathized with the first Russian Revolution, that of February, 1917; the aims of Lenin and the Bolsheviks at the time seemed to threaten a dangerous weakening of the struggle against the Central powers. I myself was not at all sure about what was going on. Only slowly, through studying intensively the literature of the Russian Revolution and Masaryk's book, *Russia and Europe*, did I begin to see, although still not clearly, that a victory of the Western powers would not be the end of the first world war. The fundamental problem for Europe went far beyond those differences which had become manifest during the war. We were standing on the threshold of yet more profound and world-shaking revolutions.

Today, looking back over the years since 1918, we see clearly that the period between the wars was only a truce, that Germany's military defeat did not lead to fundamental changes in its internal political and cultural structure, and that the Western democracies were too weak to control German nationalism, which took on, under the Nazis, grotesque and perverse forms. Berlin and Vienna fell in 1918; London and Paris dominated international relations between the two wars; and then, for a few years—from 1939 to 1945—the Nazis of Berlin and the Fascists of Rome became the masters of Europe. A second military catastrophe occurred because the leading statesmen of the West were paralysed by fear of Soviet Russia; they were incapable of understanding politically, socially, (or in the perspective of the philosophy of history) the inherent historical currents which had assumed new social and political forms in the Revolution of 1917. The second world war reduced London and Paris to the level of second-rate powers; Washington and Moscow came to express the new international situation. I might add, even though it means jumping ahead a bit, that today it is no longer just these two cities which must be considered, but also Peking. From now on, the development of our world will depend on how these three centres of world politics understand the mission of mankind and the situation of modern man.

These remarks were made in order to show the kind of realities with which we had to deal, even in our theological point of view. On the one hand, what we had to do was to work our way through to the essence of the message of the Bible. Modern theology had not penetrated to the core of biblical events or to the heart of the living Church of Christ. Traditional theology, Catholic or Protestant, had frozen the biblical message in the static forms of tradition and ecclesiastical institutions. At the same time, all of us were in some way bound up with the more superficial levels of political and national events. We had not sufficiently freed ourselves from our accustomed political ways or from our social and national, prejudices.

Even today I am continually bothered by the question of why, despite all their external historical and cultural differences, church bodies all over the world show in varying degrees a middle-class bourgeois mentality, with all its limitations and sluggishness. Why have they become firmly convinced that they are comprised of good, decent people who should not soil their hands by having anything to do with this restless, corrupt world? Why is there among them so little of the kind of discernment that might enable them to overcome the limitations of ordinary national, political and church life? Is it because we are not sufficiently anchored in the Bible? Or is it because we have not yet penetrated to the very heart of the revolutionary mystery of the Gospel? Why have the churches of the Reformation concentrated, in both theology and practice, on a few old reformation themes, whether justification by faith alone or 'soli Deo gloria'? Why have we failed to take seriously the fact that Jesus of Nazareth was thrown out of the synagogues and temples and condemned to death by scribes and priests? Why do we refuse to follow the example of Jesus who went among the lepers and outcasts and declared that he would lead into his kingdom those who fell by the wayside and lived as outcasts, and for whom no one cared? Why so little comprehension of the shocks of social revolution? And why even today, in the vast majority of churches (even in the socialist countries), such a half-hearted attempt to come to terms with the events of 1917?

These were and remain the theological questions with which I have been most preoccupied since the end of the first world war. At the same time, I have been critically analysing myself and asking whether I have really found appropriate words to express contemporary problems; I have even been asking myself whether I have correctly understood the times in which I have grown up. Even after the first world war, when I was involved in the movement for the union of Czech Protestants, I saw this movement rather as the inspiration for the liberation of the life of our nation. Although, as I have already mentioned, the social aspects of public action were very close to the centre of my concern, it was the struggle for national liberation which occupied most of my thoughts during the war years.

A challenge

But here I must modify or at least supplement my narrative. On the one hand I must draw attention to something I have already said: that studying the revolutionary literature of Russia opened my eyes to questions which went well beyond those of national freedom. In particular I must mention the experiences I had in the last year of the war, as a military chaplain. I was on the Eastern frontier of Austria, at a point where the Polish, Ukrainian and Rumanian peoples come into close contact and are intermingled in terms of language, nation and church. I was in touch with prisoners of war returning from captivity in Russia after the peace of Brest-Litovsk in the Spring of 1918. From them I was able to learn about what was taking place in revolutionary Russia. For the most part, they had not much sympathy for the revolution, but through their accounts I was able to understand even the positive aspects of the Bolshevik revolution. I related this information to my literary knowledge of the revolutionary ferment in Russia since the middle of the nineteenth century, and thus came to understand, albeit not completely clearly, that what was involved were fundamental questions about the whole of our European society.

Beneath all the horrors, cruelties and brutalities of the revolution and the onset of the civil war, I heard an ominous but clear cry that the division of the world into Central European theocratic empires and Western liberal democracies was not the last word. There is a far deeper, an abysmal division between poor and rich, between those who have economic and financial power in their hands and those who have only empty hands or educated heads. This division traverses the whole world, characterizing both victors and vanquished. That which we call the class struggle is not just a propaganda slogan or a cheap call to action. It embraces the most serious of human problems: the fight against poverty and hunger, against the humiliation and exploitation of men and nations. This is an extremely complex question which concerns not just the forms of political freedom, but genuine human equality and dignity.

I became more deeply aware of the situation of modern man at war than I had at home. In the army I was able to see that a free Czechoslovak state would have to deal with more than just new democratic and political forms and national self-determination. But it was also while in the service that I lived through the fall of the Austro-Hungarian army and the almost instantaneous loss of authority of those who only yesterday or the day before had been in command or power.

And finally, it was also during this period that I spent many an hour with the Bible, studying the Hebrew prophets in particular; trying to understand, in the light of their message, the earth-shaking historical upheavals, personal and social human poverty, and the mission of the church in the contemporary situation. And I sensed that above all the political changes, above the defeated theocratic empires of Central Europe, above the victorious Western democracies, and above the tumultuous revolutionary events in nearby Russia, the Lord of life and death reigned. Out of the sovereignty of his love and mercy he is present among us, to set us our tasks and guide our steps.

I felt an unbounded happiness

The Republic of Czechoslovakia was born on October 28, 1918. I did not personally experience the enthusiasm of the Czech and Slovak people at the break-up of the Empire because I was still away in the East near the Russian border where I spent the last months and days of the war as a military chaplain. Even so, I was forced by circumstances to assume command of the camp for a few days, clear evidence that the officers of the crumbling Empire had completely lost all their authority and control over the soldiers. In such instances, where discipline came to an end, there was the danger of chaos and bloody conflict. The Czech soldiers were relatively among the most disciplined and helped maintain order in the camp. This was probably the result of the fact that we had the clearest ideas about the future organization and political life we wanted for our country. T. G. Masaryk triumphed because of the clarity of his programme and because of his deep roots in the traditions of Czech politics and his knowledge of international affairs. German soldiers from Austria were depressed; those from Germany disoriented; and the others had only vague ideas about what could grow up on the ground of the former monarchies.

In early November I returned to my own country, where I terminated my work as assistant pastor of the congregation at Salvator Church in Prague and prepared myself for independent work in the congregation of Sonov to which I had meanwhile been called. I can no longer recall today exactly how I felt in this early period of the new Czechoslovakia. My impressions were not all of one kind. On one hand I felt an unbounded happiness that the ancient Czech state had been reborn, this time in connection with the Slovak section of old Hungary, and that at the head of our country stood a man whose spiritual and political thought was internationally known. And related to this was a pleasure that the Hussite and Lutheran churches of Czech Protestantism were preparing to unite into the Evangelical Church of Czech Brethren. This actually took place on December 17 and 18, 1918. But on the other hand, I could not help wondering whether we would be strong enough, politically and morally, to overcome the enormous historical shock caused by the fall of the old Empire.

A certain void

For centuries the area of Europe from the Krkonose (Giant mountains) and Tatra mountains to the Adriatic Sea had been under the rule of imperial Vienna. The differences among the Czech, Hungarian and Yugoslav lands were great, but even so there existed a common tradition—one that was not just administrative, but also spiritual, which gave to all these lands and peoples a certain psychological unity. It was only later that we began to realize that we former citizens of the old Empire, regardless of our national origins, all shared something in our mental outlook; there was something we all had in common in our view of the world around us. In contrast to neighbouring Germany, Old Austria was often characterized as a country with a certain frivolity, a pleasant easy-goingness (*Schlamperei*), a joy in life and its gifts; there was none of the iron discipline or rigidity of Germany, nor its tenacious expansionist direction towards the future. The very foundations of Habsburg society trembled under the shock of the national awakening of the various peoples of the old Empire. It was an area where remnants of feudalism still persisted, of a theocratic atmosphere, of nationalist liberalism, progressive humanism, and, of course, also of the revolutionary currents of socialism. But all these national, political and social forces were formed by ancient social and cultural traditions. In fact the demise of the Empire created a certain void and the course of European politics between the wars was marked to a degree by the conflicts among the new states that emerged on the ruins of Austria-Hungary. At the time, however, our analysis of the situation was not sufficiently thorough.

Thus it was only gradually that we also came to realize that coexistence between the Czechs and the Slovaks was not to prove as simple as we had thought it would be. The cultural

31

and social structure of old Hungary left its mark on the Slovaks, who had lived for centuries in a close relationship with the Hungarian peoples. It was necessary to have a finger on the pulse of our two peoples in order to discern the serious problems standing in the way of the Czechs and the Slovaks living together. The outset of the political life of the new state was characterized by an idyllic joy in the recent liberation, a certain lack of political experience, and a carefree certainty that we were standing on the threshold of a long era of peaceful progress. As I have already said, Masaryk brought to our society a ferment of universalism and some profound thinking. But even he, for a long time, was convinced that ahead of us lay a long period of peaceful coexistence in Europe.

In the meantime, however, new explosive materials were building up in the East, while the more destructive propensities of German nationalism were re-emerging in the West. The peace treaties of 1919–1920 proved a fragile foundation for the post-war reorganization of Europe. None of the leading French, British or American statesmen sufficiently appreciated the size of the problems facing modern man; they did not take seriously either the Russian Revolution of 1917 or the symptoms of the pathological excitement in the soul of the offended and defeated Germans. In other words, perhaps they sensed the dynamic of the Russian Revolution and the pathological fanaticism of the German people, but they believed that these two cataclysmic problems of post-war Europe could be handled by means of force. I do not wish to pass judgment: we were all too weak intellectually, spiritually, or politically to be able to control the underground chaos and the hidden forces of post-war Europe. But now, from the perspective of today, we can see fully how the year 1914 and the Revolution of 1917 were the beginnings of tremendous upheavals in the old structure of Europe and in the world order. Even today we have not yet sufficiently examined the problems—political, social and spiritual—of Europe and the West (not to mention the events and upheavals that have taken place in the wake of the second world war).

For me, Masaryk's political line was clear, and I was convinced that his social and ethical humanism would be strong enough to handle our domestic Czecho-German questions. From the outset the three million Germans who lived within the borders of our republic represented a threat to the peaceful political and cultural progress of our country, situated in the centre of an ennervated, socially and nationally divided Europe. The end of the war left Europe in the midst of a morass of crucial, but still unresolved political and social questions. But we believed that Masaryk's leadership would enable us to overcome the danger of renewed conflict and at least show the way in which not just our country but the whole of Europe should strive to bring the German problem under control and form the basis for a creative understanding of the Bolshevik Revolution. This was no light task; it may even have been an impossible one. Europe was in such a crisis, politically, socially, nationally and spiritually, that she could not longer fulfil her grand mission. Nor, probably, has she been in a position to do so since; for we are now even more frightened by the possibility that the second world catastrophe may have carried us yet further in these directions. We know from private sources that Masaryk was deeply disturbed by growing German nationalism even in the 1920s. We shared his concern about the failure of the majority of German Protestants to understand the consequences of the German defeat in 1918 and how such a failure might render the peaceful development of the Weimar Republic impossible. Masaryk also had realistic plans for the social reconstruction of the life of our nation. But he was not decisive or strong enough to help bring revolutionary Russia and its Soviet government into the community of Europe and the rest of the world. In the 'twenties—and even more so later on—we saw that without open and positive co-operation with Soviet Russia, it would be impossible to preserve peace or settle any of the fundamental questions of the post-war world.

The truth which comes from above

It may seem that I am talking too much about political and international questions. I should point out, however, that all these questions were—in this period when my theological thought was maturing—bound up with ecclesiastical and theological struggles, and that for several years these burdensome questions were one of my two primary preoccupations ... As I look back on the 'twenties, I see three areas into which my theological efforts were directed.

In the first place there was a struggle—once again with Masaryk's philosophical and religious work. Masaryk was a child of the nineteenth century in his rationalism and positivism and his attempts to grasp the Christian faith in terms of its temporal, cultural, rational and ethical consequences. I was fascinated by his analysis of the religious crisis of modern man; his studies on the titanism of the nineteenth century, from Goethe's *Faust* and Musset through the romanticism of Byron and Lermontov up to Nietzsche, remain, in our literature, unforgettable documents of how modern man, in all seriousness, penetrated through to the core of the so-called religious problem. In the titanism of Faust Masaryk saw the struggle of the individual against everything which is received as objectively true and binding. Masaryk fought subjectivism and all attempts to reduce ethical norms and intellectual truths to the level of products of the external world or to make the human subject the source of all truth and ethical norms. Man is not his own master. Masaryk was extremely critical of those tendencies which have resulted in contemporary existentialism. But his almost existential opposition to revealed religion—that is, to the belief that God reveals himself to man through his incarnation and his Word—was evidence that Masaryk had not extricated himself from the idea that human personality, by its intellectual and moral activity and by its consciousness of its responsibility, was the supreme authority in the order of spiritual values. In his study on Dostoevsky, written in the early 1890s, and his analysis of the philosophy of J. V. Kireesvsky, Masaryk seems to have reached the threshold of what we call revelation. But all his later philosophy dealing with religion rejected more and more clearly everything which classical Christianity has always seen as the basic source and foundation of faith and life. My struggle over Masaryk's authority in political and cultural life went side by side with searching but positive criticism of his religious philosophy.

One of Masaryk's most remarkable followers, Emmanuel Radl, saw that Masaryk was too static a philosopher, that his ethical rationalism rendered him incapable of hearing what in the Old and New Testaments was the starting point of all thought, that which has given our civilization its distinctive character. Masaryk also seemed to Radl to be a man who wanted to be master of philosophy and of truth, that he lacked that open, frank relationship to the truth which comes from above and impels us to serve both God and our fellow men. My collaboration with Radl, a professor of philosophy, was one of my deepest experiences, one from which I gained much more than I gave.

When we speak the name of God

I have already noted how my theological and philosophical thinking was firmly rooted in our local traditions and nourished by Central European problems. Nevertheless, I cannot overlook the foreign theological influences—especially those of Switzerland and Germany—which penetrated my life and the life of our community. And at this point I shall return to my remarks about my student years. For in spite of my close bonds with my own church and with our national and political traditions, in spite of all the attention I paid to men like T. G. Masaryk or E. Radl, I eagerly welcomed the impetus of theological change then coming from Switzerland, from men like Hermann Kutter and Leonard Ragaz.

These two had been part of my theological growth even before the first world war, but their voices became urgent for me during the inter-war period. In their work I became certain that the Word of the God of Israel and of Jesus Christ intervenes overwhelmingly in human history; that what is involved is not mere personal religious experiences or private piety, but rather an upheaval in the whole life of society. Much later a line was drawn, in theology, between religion and biblical faith, between the psychic process of religion and the objective intervention of the living God in human history. To be sure, Kutter and Ragaz—under the influence of the Blumhardts, father and son—liberated theology from the religious romanticism identified with names like Schleiermacher and different theological schools. When we speak the name of God we are not invoking a mere human feeling or religious mood; what is involved is a revolutionary upheaval in men's lives. And when we say Jesus Christ, we mean that God reigns in history and determines both public and private life. The Gospel is not just the sweetness of personal consolation through the remission of guilt and sin, but rather the reign of the living God who leads redeemed sinners into the struggle against hypocrisy and sterility, against rigid ecclesiastical institutions, and against the loss of suffering, hunger, sickness and poverty in all human situations.

All these men opened the eyes of us divinity students to the reality that the Gospel of Jesus of Nazareth transcends the limits of church institutions, and that it may even be hidden, but at work, in movements which seem to be directed against religion or the Church. And that which we call revelation acquired a new urgency in our thinking and in the moments of decision, and became the foundation and starting-point of our theology.

The voice of Karl Barth

It is here that the initiative of the revolutionary theology of Karl Barth, Eduard Thurneysen, and their collaborators, fit in. I accepted Barth's influence with an open mind once I had become aware that modern pre-war theology was already insufficient for dealing with the war-time and post-war upheavals. Pre-war theology had been too much tied up with the peaceful development of Europe during that period; it had grown up from the ground of Central European academic intellectualism, and failed to search into the depths of human weakness or the chasms of the political and social divisions that were developing beneath the surface of the apparent calm. What is the mission of the living Church of Christ? Is it just to supply 'religion' and make national and social life more beautiful? Should it deal only with so-called religious needs and restrict its scope to a limited area of life which has its own necessities, and ignore the rest of social, political, scientific or cultural life? Or is its mission rather to preach to this world, in all its complexity and division, the message which proclaims from on high, unconditionally and inescapably, a pardoning grace, a judgment on man and on the world?

The starting-point of Barth's theology was not that of academic questions, but rather a question about the Church, about its purpose and its mission in the world. I was aware from the outset that Barth's voice was more than just a despairing cry emerging from the ruins of the post-war world. Even though his theology used to be interpreted as a response to the disorder of contemporary society and culture, as a kind of flight from the crisis of the times to the refuge of biblical authority and concentration on the Church, it was clear to me that the deepest motives of this theological struggle were a positive and energetic attempt to capture the actual meaning of the biblical Word, the actual themes of the Old and New Testaments, and the fundamental task of the community of the Church in the midst of a disturbed and agitated world. It dealt with something that modern theology had failed to grasp because it had shut up the living and shattering Word in a rigid dogmatic system and in ecclesiastical institutions.

Barth's theology was no flight from the scientific methods of theology, from critical thought, from an uneasy world. It was a critical struggle for a reality which transcends human intellectual, philosophical, social and political categories. It was in this daring and positive determination that I saw the real, and special meaning of Barth's theological struggle, a struggle which was later to have a fundamental significance in that fateful crisis of German Protestantism, the Nazi period. It was necessary to penetrate to the actual core of the Bible and descend to the very foundations of the living Church if theology was to return to its essential function and become a creative force in the lives of men caught up in the tempestuous social and political waves of the time.

We saw the limitations

Barth's theology was a corrective to Ragaz's religious socialism. There was a certain danger in the work of Kutter and Ragaz that the core of biblical and church life would be prematurely transformed into social and political pathos. But, on the other hand, there was another danger, perhaps even greater, that Barth's crisis or dialectical theology, later transformed into a church theology, would become a school; that it would become too systematized, and that its adherents would be deprived of the chance of viewing freshly the ever new upheavals of history. What we tried to do was to accept Barth's influences along with Kutter's and Ragaz's emphases. Ragaz remained for us the light by which we viewed the limitations of every theological system and every ecclesiastical institution. We had to save something of the dynamic of history from Ragaz for the new struggles and tasks of the Church.

Then, too, in looking back, there is always, for me, the question of whether the broad perspective of Ernst Troeltsch was not lost too quickly in the new situation of post-war Germany. Troeltsch, of course, abdicated from the realm of theology and died prematurely in 1923. His theology died out because it lost the biblical heart of all missionary theology. As a theologian he was bound to be displaced by Barth. But I cannot help wondering whether, during the 'twenties when nationalism dominated the churches and theology schools of Germany, and when only a very few German Protestants understood the meaning and results of the first world war, the fall of the imperial monarchy, and the defeat of German aggression, Troeltsch might not have been able to influence German thinking more effectively than could those theological groups centred around Barth's work. Such a question of course, can only be asked from today's perspective.

It is hardly necessary to emphasize what Barth meant during the years of struggle for the German churches, especially from 1933–35. At that time Barth really entered, in a creative way, into the history of the Church. But those who were guided, in the Confessing Church (*Bekennende Kirche*), by Barth's influence often concentrated only on questions of the confession of faith and the existence of the Church; they did not understand the problem of German history, which resulted so catastrophically in the second world war. In my opinion, the voices of Barth, Ragaz and Troeltsch still survive and make themselves felt in theological discussions. I should only like to add that these influences also affected us, though within the context of our own theological and cultural traditions.

CATHOLICISM AND THE STRUGGLE FOR CHRISTIANITY

The Catholic influence

The third aspect of my activity between the wars deserves special attention: it was a theological and cultural effort to deepen my understanding of the Catholic Church and of Catholic theology. The first years after the birth of the independence of Czechoslovakia were marked by an intense antipathy towards any influence on the part of the Catholic Church. This is historically and psychologically understandable. The victory of the Catholic Church, led by the Hapsburgs, in 1620, brought with it the end of our national independence and the liquidation of the heritage of Hus and the Reformation. The next one-hundred-and-sixty years (until the Edict of Toleration) were years of national humiliation that had a definite Catholic hue, in the form of counter-reformation Jesuit Catholicism.

My impression even today is that this counter-reformation

Catholicism did not achieve a transformation of the inner lives of the Czechs; that their 'recatholicization' was to a considerable extent the result partly of force, but most of all an effort to escape into a superficial religiosity. This is not to say that the last three hundred years produced nothing in Czech Catholicism worthy of note or respect. There were several fine Catholics who participated in our national revival, men like F. Dobrovsky and B. Bolzano. But the Catholic Church bore the mark of feudalism, of its position as the official state church, of external—superficial—formalism, yes, of superstition.

The nineteenth century was marked by vehement protests against Catholic domination in education and upbringing, and against the reactionary Catholic dream of keeping the Czech people submissive to the dynasty in Vienna and to Austrian patriotism. The fall of the Austro-Hungarian monarchy deeply affected the structure of the whole Catholic Church. In early November, 1918, the statue of the Virgin Mary, Our Lady of Victory, in Prague's Old City Square, was demolished—it had been considered a symbol both of the triumph of Catholicism and of the national humiliation of the Czech people. The slogan that after the defeat of Vienna we must free ourselves from Rome spread from mouth to mouth and influenced the entire atmosphere of our national culture. From a historical perspective all this was understandable—a morally and psychologically inevitable step. It was a rebellion against the three hundred years' old heritage of the lost battle of White Mountain (1620).

Even so, it was clear to all intellectuals and responsible citizens of the young republic that such an attitude could not be allowed to be the last word. Vulgar national political slogans were not enough in working out the relationships between modern Czechoslavakia and the Catholic Church. The essence of Catholicism cannot be identified with the politics of a feudal reactionary Austria, with cultural backwardness, or with superstitious cults based on places of pilgrimage. In theology and philosophy, in culture and in art, morally and religiously, Catholicism established the structure of European thinking. Catholicism is St Augustine, St Thomas Aquinas, St Francis of Assisi, Dante Alighieri, the saints of the Middle Ages, the Spaniard Cervantes and the whole gallery of Spanish mystics, not to mention the various representatives of Catholic art and poetry in all the countries of Europe.

As a Protestant theologian I anxiously asked myself if a superficial anti-clerical attitude would not deprive our intellectual and spiritual life of some essential aspects of European civilization. But I also asked myself whether we Protestants were not depriving ourselves, by our anti-Catholic sentiment of a really deep understanding of what the leaders of the Reformation from Jan Hus and Petr Chelčicky up to Jan Amos Komensky (Comenius) had struggled and suffered for. I was convinced that the heart of the Reformation could be understood and preserved only by coming to terms in depth with that which made a Catholic Catholic, with that which expressed the basic character of Catholicism: its liturgy of the Mass—the Eucharist—and its special understanding of the Gospel

Thus by the early 'twenties I was already attempting to draw attention, first in journals and then in books, to the intellectual and spiritual losses which we were in danger of incurring through vulgar anti-Catholicism. At the same time, I presented in my theological analyses the essence of classical Catholicism and its creative historical role. I do not know whether I always found the right words or method in the course of these efforts, for I encountered a marked lack of comprehension both within my own church as well as among various progressive circles which had been otherwise politically close to me. But I did find full understanding on the part of my collaborator, Emmanuel Radl who, as an older companion, was my inspiring teacher and counsellor. In 1925 my book *Catholicism and the Struggle for Christianity* was published, and two years later I founded with Radl *The Christian Review* so as to be able to present to the Czech public our theological, philosophical and ecclesiastical opinions in relation to the needs of our political and cultural life. It was also an attempt to awaken our Christians to ecumenical thinking and the transcending of the frontiers between Protestantism, Catholicism and Orthodoxy. We were not just trying to overcome sterile anti-Catholic and anti-church tendencies; we sought, by analysing actual classical Christianity, to discover the place where living faith—Catholic and Protestant—emerges, based on the transfiguring, revolutionary witness of the prophets and apostles.

Looking ahead

Our task was not easy, one of the reasons being that Catholicism from the beginning of this century had lived in a strong anti-modern, anti-ecumenical atmosphere. At the time our publishing activity in *The Christian Review* began, Pope Pius XI had just published, in January, 1928, his Encyclical, *Mortalium Animos*, directed against ecumenism. This document in many places silenced those voices which had been coming out in favour of spiritual contact among the various Christian faiths. The Roman Church was still a fortress against the modern world and against everything that went beyond the strict forms of dogma, the liturgy, canon law or piety. We did not let ourselves be disconcerted, however, and we were able in some measure to foresee that the time would come when even the Catholic Church would loosen the rigidity of its forms, unbolt its rusted lock and keys, and begin listening to those voices coming perhaps from other churches but which, in the last analysis, had something to offer even to the Catholic Church. I was convinced that the anti-modernism of Pius X could lay the basis for an intensive return to the actual sources of faith (to revelation), and to that which we can, appropriately, call the mystery of the Gospel. The liturgical movement, represented primarily by the Benedictines, returned to the liturgical forms of the ancient Christians and awakened an interest even in non-Latin rites. The efforts to restore the original themes of St Augustine broke through the sterile scholasticism of St Thomas and brought fresh air to all the rooms still musty with medieval theology. A whole range of excellent Catholic writers in Europe and America (and in Czechoslovakia as well) were evidence that even in the Catholic fortress, barricaded against the world, the real life of faith was boiling over and that Catholicism in its original form was still the source of a creative upsurge.

As a Protestant theologian I was also impressed by the fact that, while the majority of German Protestants, with their sterile resistance to the Weimar Republic, aided the restorationist and nationalist forces of destruction, German Catholics had the courage to assume the responsibility for the life of the new state which had arisen on the ruins of imperial monarchy. I am not dealing here, of course, with the shortcomings and errors of the German Catholic *Zentrum*. However, I do look at the events of the inter-war period as a whole, and I see how German Catholicism was politically more mature and better prepared for the tasks of building the new state than was Protestantism.

This effort to understand more deeply the Catholic faith, its theology and its church, prepared me for the changes which occurred in Catholicism under Pope John XXIII and as a result of the Second Vatican Council. But I cannot say how disappointed I was when, in 1936, several Czech Catholic writers, from whom I had expected far profounder historical foresight and political wisdom, took the side of the Spanish counter-revolution.

THE ORTHODOX CHURCH AND THE SOVIETS

A permanent loss

We thought a great deal, during these years, about the situation of the Orthodox Church in the Soviet Union. I experienced a kind of inner struggle. As I have already re-marked, the October Revolution of 1917 represented for me an irreversible turning-point of history; it was, moreover, an event that in one way or another was bound to have an effect on our own social and cultural activity. I well understood that much of the suffering of our Orthodox brothers in the Soviet Union sprang from social and political grounds. The church could not escape the results of its close relationship with the Tsarist monarchy and the whole socio-political structure of pre-revolutionary Russia. The church was totally unprepared for the Revolution and during the civil war sided more or less with the counter-revolution.

Even so, I was anxious lest the disruption of the Orthodox Church result in irreparable spiritual, moral and even cultural and political damage. Many of the leading Orthodox intellec-tuals left revolutionary Russia, some voluntarily and some against their will. I became personally acquainted with some of them; through conversations and reading their books I sought to answer the question as to whether or not their departure meant a permanent loss for Soviet society. Nikolai Berdyaev, Sergei Bulgakov, N. Arseniev, L. A. Zander, Georges Florovsky, Glubokovsky and many others were among them. I was very much drawn, in reading the revolutionary literature of Russia, towards the revolutionary democratic thinking of men like Belinsky, Herzen and Chernyshevsky, but my interest did not stop with them. I know how progressive Russian society condemned Gogol because of his adherence to Orthodoxy, and how Dostoevsky remains a controversial figure even for contemporary Soviet people. But I still believe that one cannot think of the future of Soviet society without hoping that that which is represented by Gogol and Dostoevsky, Kireevsky, and Solovyov will play a creative role in the spiritual efforts of contemporary Soviet society, but with full understanding of the revolutionary upheavals that have taken place in Russia.

Those who left Russia after the Revolution represent a whole gamut of beliefs and social and political aspirations. I knew personally Metropolitan Antony (Khrapovistky) who deliberately excluded himself from the new socialist state by virtue of his reactionary—not just conservative—views. But I also knew Nikolai Berdyaev, who, shortly before his death in Paris, confessed to me how he longed to return to post-revolutionary Russia.

Russia's spiritual life

The question of how the Orthodox Church, which over the last fifty years has done little more than cling to its naked existence in the framework of its hierarchy, its liturgy and its sacraments, can enter creatively into today's Soviet society and bring to it the living heritage of its history, remains a particularly difficult question. I fervently hope that the Russian Orthodox Church will become an active participant in theological, ecumenical and spiritual discussions with the Catholic, Protestant and Anglican Churches.

When I mention the possibility that members of the Russian Orthodox Church can become a creative force in the development of Soviet society, I do not in the least envisage the return of Russia to pre-revolutionary times. The changes that have taken place since then in education, culture, the economy and in social and political affairs have penetrated so deeply into the inner structure of the Soviet peoples, that there is no sense in even talking about any return to the past. But history is a complex process, involving both external and internal spiritual life. We who live in the context of the attempts in East Europe to build socialism are not only experiencing personally the unity of socialist purposes and goals, but at the same time we are becoming aware wherein we differ from each other according to our spiritual traditions and the conditions in which we grew up. Just as our spiritual life bears the imprint of its Catholic or Protestant and Hussite past, so Russia's is marked by centuries of Orthodox history, by its ways of thinking, its liturgy and sacraments, its mystic iconography, and its idea of the Church as the essential precondition of personal life and faith. The longer Soviet society lasts the more positively it will evaluate the spiritual accomplishments of the past, whether in art and literature, or in religious and ecclesiastical traditions. To be sure, the official anti-religious ideology has not disappeared, and so-called atheistic propaganda has been kept up, though at times artificially. But even from the spiritual standpoint, today's Soviet man needs something far more positive and creative than the mere negation of faith and religion, of the Church and its traditions. For those who would

47

know contemporary Russian communism, the textbook study of Marx's concepts, or even of Lenin's writings is far from sufficient. To understand Soviet Russian society properly, it is necessary to understand Russian history from the beginnings of Christianity and its tragic struggles against the Mongol-Tartar invasions and oppression, as well as against the West, represented by the Baltic Germans and Swedes or by the Poles and the Lithuanians.

Even Russian communism, while its roots lie in the Marxist movement in the West, is profoundly influenced by the struggles of the Russian spirit in the fields of politics and society, literature and philosophy. All the great progressive movements, from the Decembrists (1825) and Petrashev Group (1848) up through the various socialist groups at the turn of the present century have influenced the structure of the Russian Revolution. Without Belinsky and Herzen, but also without Pushkin and Lermontov, Tolstoi and Gorky, we cannot understand what is emerging even in today's Soviet man. Let us not forget what I pointed out above, that even Dostoevsky with his impressive grasp of the conflicts of the human spirit on the border between faith and unbelief, his love for those who suffer, are insulted or oppressed, unhappy or afflicted, hungry or poor, helped to prepare the rebellion against official society, against the cold selfishness of the wealthy, and, yes, even against the official church with its rigid formalism and its blindness to the deep suffering of the people of Russia. It was not for nothing that Merezkovsky called him the prophet of the Russian Revolution.

Gold from the rocks

But why do I write all this? I wish to present the viewpoint from which I was able to come to terms with the Russian

Revolution, without seeing communism just as some abstract ideological system or as the violent overthrow of an established order by a small band of the Voluhoranes. Moral conflicts, the problems of supremacy, of justice and of the relationship between the individual and society, the place of personality in history, can be understood in Russian (as in any other) communism only when we take account of history and discover the links between today and the rich and creative traditions of preceding generations. Neither the Revolution nor the Civil War is the last word. After the destruction of the old state and social order comes a time of systematic building when responsible people hunt eagerly for everything in their history which was creative, when they extract gold from the rocks or the sand-beds of rivers. If we cannot be exact in our forecasts, it is yet possible to envisage a time when even the Eastern Orthodox Churches will come to play a significant role in a developed socialist society. After years of flight behind the walls of ancient hierarchical and liturgical forms, after years of resignation and a fatalistic view of the future, the time will come when it becomes increasingly clear that not even communists are the only or final architects of the future, that the future depends also on Christians and on their daring vision of a society of citizens, free, responsible and dedicated to the public service.

I have read Masaryk's classic *Russia and Europe* (the English version is entitled *The Spirit of Russia*) several times, with great attention and profit. But it seems to me that the author re-remained imprisoned within the limitations of nineteenth-century rationalistic humanism and that he was thus unable to grasp the full, abysmic depth of the situation of a Christian today, of mankind today, in a period of terrifying revolutionary upheaval and the painful building of a new social order.

EUROPE'S CRISIS: A TEST OF THEOLOGY

Still we hoped

Thus we reached the terrible crisis which engulfed Europe and the whole human race at the end of the 'thirties. For me, this crisis, especially where it concerned the Western parts of Europe, was not just a shattering political question, but also a fundamental enigma of history, philosophy and even theology. It may be that we were too naïve in our view of the international situation, but for a long time we believed that the victors of 1918 were going to be strong, prudent and intelligent enough, after winning the war, to be able to preserve peace.

I already mentioned above that I had long been disturbed by the lack of understanding, on the part of the leading European statesmen and politicians, of the Revolution of 1917 and the existence of a socialist Russia. Even so, however, I believed that Western civilization would not permit another resort to force, one that sought to disrupt the Europe that had been organized in the Peace Treaties of 1919 and 1920. The British Empire with its invincible Navy, France with its Army—considered the strongest in Europe—and the United States with its boundless wealth seemed firm guarantees of peace against the counter-revolutionary Nazi Germany and the Fascist Italy. London and Paris determined the direction of international affairs and ensured the firm ground of the international order. The existence of my country depended on the solidity of the West. It was in the context of this hope that we undertook our theological work, took part in ecumenical relations and contacts, sought firm foundations for theology and the Church, and fought for the humanitarian democracy of Masaryk against the pettiness of nationalism and bourgeois selfishness.

But still we hoped that the Soviet Union could be brought

into the arena of international co-operation and its socialism be activated as a fruitful ferment in the struggle against a growing political reaction and cowardly conservatism.

Applauding Germany's politics

In our neighbouring countries, however, destructive currents of national and political brutality were growing, of a sort that we had not imagined even in our most horrible nightmares. Not just the majority of Western statesmen, but wide ranges of Western society were much more paralysed by fear of Eastern communism than by the counter-revolution in Central Europe.

By way of excuse we can of course mention certain things that took place in Soviet society—especially the shocking purges of the late 'thirties—but not even they can explain the spiritual torpor, the political and even social paralysis of the West. This is hard for me to understand even today, even though the study of sociology and psychology has enabled me to understand various things. And to this day I am shaken by the horrible role played by the German people under the leadership of Hitler, by their bloody suppression of political opponents during time of peace, and by their monstrous liquidation of their Jewish fellow citizens. An educated nation, proud of its science and philosophy, its technical development and organizational capacity, let itself be pulled down to hitherto unimaginable depths of cruelty, vindictiveness and nihilism. And let us not forget that there were many thousands, if not millions, in the neighbouring countries who, actively or tacitly, applauded Germany's politics in the hope that it would offer a means to overcome the danger of communism in the East.

Who could thenceforth avoid doubting whether modern civilization, with its science, its technology, and its organization, was in fact leading mankind to ever higher levels of happiness, welfare, progress and peaceful coexistence? Who could stop and halt a nation which had used armed power and economic strength, wantonly and ruthlessly, against those who were weaker and poorer? I was forced to struggle with these questions from a theological viewpoint. I began to doubt the health and spiritual trustworthiness of so-called Western civilization.

It was precisely during the worst period of this world crisis that I became increasingly convinced that the efforts of Soviet Russia were going to have a creative significance for the future style of men's lives and for the building of an international society. Only in 1940–41 I was deeply concerned lest, under the pressure of the military situation after the fall of France, the Soviet Union would seek a false peace with the temporary victors and with Japan. This anxiety was short-lived, however, and I mention it only by way of pointing out the vicissitudes of my inner struggle. Despite my esteem and respect for the Confessing Church in Germany, disturbing questions arose within me as to whether its theological wisdom was sufficiently penetrating to permit it a sane orientation in the international military and spiritual confusion of the time. The fall of democratic Czechoslovakia in 1938–39 shocked us not only politically but also spiritually, and meant for us the end of one epoch without any clear view of what our new beginnings would be like.

A Diagnosis of German Protestantism

Subjectivism

It was understandable that in such a situation we returned to the very foundations of our theology, that we even asked if there were not some fundamental error in the Lutheran Reformation which was responsible for what had happened in

Germany. During the 'twenties German Protestantism had tried to come to a new and deeper understanding of Luther's spiritual efforts and of his conception of the Church. It was one of the post-war currents which sought to revise the theological liberalism of the last century and, with it, the traditional Lutheran confessionalism.

At that time we were all thinking very seriously about the true motives of Luther's return to the biblical message and, especially, to Paul's conception of the Gospel. We were impressed by Luther's energy in laying bare, beneath the deposits of church tradition and theological speculation, the shattering message of the sovereignty of the God of grace and mercy in Jesus Christ. From this viewpoint, Luther remains for us even today one of the most impressive revealers of Paul's approach to the Gospel. But even at the time we were disturbed by Luther's excessive subjectivism, by his concentration on the inner experience of justification and reconciliation, on inner defiance and by the almost superhuman boldness with which he spoke of the certainty of salvation. Luther is, perhaps, one of the sources of German subjectivism, a subjectivism which knows how to penetrate to the furthest depths of man and to the highest reaches of the spiritual experiences of redemption and salvation, but that at the same time neglects all that is going on around it, the role the Church must undertake in order that human relationships in society may become more just and sensitive to the needs of the most humble levels of society? What is concerned here are two historical realities of fateful consequences.

The thesis of the two kingdoms

Luther never mastered, theologically or from the point of view of the Church, that which in Catholicism is called *potestas jurisdictionis*, or, in contemporary terms, the autonomous construction of a church order, independent from the state, and the responsibility of the Church for freedom, justice and social humanism in the world.

Suddenly, in the light of events in the Third Reich, and in the life of the Church as well, we experienced graphically the unfortunate consequences of Luther's thesis of the two kingdoms, the one that of the Church where the principles of the reign of Christ hold sway, and the other that of temporal life where the law of Christ has no place and where political, economic, social or cultural laws are sovereign. I do not wish to criticize this theory lightly, because I know how difficult it is to detect the authority of the Gospel of Christ in public life. I also know how naïvely some Christians take the affirmation that Christ reigns over the whole world. But when we considered the impotence of the Protestant confessions *vis à vis* political events, and when we saw how easily a deeply religious inner life and a total lack of interest in the situation of the world could go together, we began asking whether this alliance might not have its roots in Luther himself. This became a particularly poignant question when we saw how easily the Church became an instrument of the powers of this world.

For these reasons, we turned with a genuine and attentive interest to our own Czech reformation traditions. As has already been said, Luther's decision in 1525 against the peasantry during the Peasant Wars, stifled any inclination on the part of the German people to understand the real motives of revolution or resistance to the authorities of the existing order when the latter undertake tyrannical and ruthless measures against their so-called subjects. The history of our reformation began with an ardent concern for the poor and the lowly (Milic of Kromeriz, 1374). Hus's reformation never became an affair of the upper classes, of the princes and nobles, but rather involved the broad masses, evoking the enthusiasm and following of ordinary people both in the towns and in the countryside. The impassioned struggle for the authority of Christ was a struggle to realize his reign in the Church and in the world. Faith was, to be sure, a joyful reliance on grace, but at the same time an obedience and responsibility in following in the way of Christ. The leaders of our reformation did not concentrate one-sidedly on their own inner lives, but rather listened both to what came from above and to what was taking place here below. Our reformation churches could never become fixed institutions, assured of their political place and sanctified by tradition. Instead they were like the people of the convenant, on the way (*communio viatorum*). Their perspective was ever forward, fixed on the final victory of Christ, so that they were able to overcome the dangers of religious and intellectual subjectivism. All this helped us during the 1930s and '40s, while the events of those years also brought us to a theologically deeper and spiritually more responsible understanding of the legacy of our reformation traditions. Needless to say, we thus also became aware of the weaknesses of our reformation as well as of our church and political life.

I do not intend, with these remarks, to elevate self-consciously and self-righteously the traditions of the Czech Reformation and sink to the level of celebrating our own history and nation. All I wish is to show, in a few words, how even my own theological efforts and self-awareness were influenced by the historical situation. It became increasingly clear to me that our theological efforts and our work in building the Church had to grow out of our own traditions, and not be a mere passive reflection of what was going on in German or Swiss theology. But even here I emphasize the significance of the historical situation, not so that history might transform the message of the Bible, of the prophets and the apostles, but rather so that we might more deeply understand the meaning of the fact that God has come into our lives in the body of a particular Man at a particular time and place, that he is the lord not only of the Church but of the whole world around us, and that we thus may undertake our work in the joyous hope of his final victory.

All this protected us from falling into the view which sees religion as a subjective self-assertion, and from the intellectual titanism of philosophy and politics. The shattering crisis of the 'thirties, during which the very existence of our nation was at stake, forced us to reconsider the bases of our historical, political and spiritual traditions. We knew that our future was uncertain, but we set out to determine, by serious study and energetic self-criticism, whether we, as a small nation, had any mission in the centre of Europe, and what was the content of our vital national traditions. And in doing this, we had to go back to the roots of our reformation struggles as well as of the theology behind them.

Looking history in the face

We—and especially I—were reproached for being too much concerned with history, and for permitting the impact of history—of the philosophy of history—to influence our spiritual efforts. However, this was a result of the peculiar position we occupied in Central Europe. Consider the profound changes we have been through during the last few centuries! More than once they involved us in serious political struggle, which put in jeopardy the very life of our nation.

Czech Catholicism no longer has a direct link with the Catholicism of the Middle Ages. It was shaped rather by the

Counter-Reformation and its efforts to recapture the souls of the Czech people by secondary religious methods: the cult of the Virgin Mary, various places of pilgrimage, and Baroque sentimentality. And we Protestants had also lost any organic relationship with the times of Hus and the Reformation. Our history is filled with dynamism and explosiveness. No sooner had we acquired national and political independence than we found ourselves facing the mortal danger of the Nazi counter-revolution, which sought to destroy everything by which the people of central Europe lived and every influence of Christianity on the structure of European civilization. It was not easy to master this historical process. This is why we had to go beyond the boundaries of purely academic study and look history directly in the face. We learnt from the experiences of the theologians and churches of central Europe, of Germany and of Switzerland, and we listened to the voices coming from Holland and France; we established contact with English and Scottish churches, but even so we were constantly forced to grapple with questions that grew up from the depths and convulsions of our own situation.

THREE

American Victory in the
Years of Chaos

1939–47

THE FALL OF CZECHOSLOVAKIA in 1939 and the occupation
of the country by the Nazis forced me to go, via Geneva and
Paris, to the United States. Throughout the war and for two
years thereafter I taught at Princeton Theological Seminary.
The ecumenical centre in Geneva, in particular its head, W. A.
Visser't Hooft, did everything possible to facilitate my family's
move to America.

AMERICAN THEOLOGICAL AND POLITICAL DILEMMAS

The terrain

At Princeton I became closely associated with John A.
Mackay, a remarkable man who combined the living tradition
of Scottish Presbyterianism, austere yet subtly poetic, with
Spanish culture, learnt through his personal knowledge of the
mystics of the seventeenth century, from the tradition of
Cervantes to that of Unamuno. His theology was—and still
is—shot through with a powerful personal experience of
pietism, in the best sense of the term, a poetic refinement, and
an extraordinary openness to all intellectual and spiritual
phenomena, on the border between the Church and the
world, theology and philosophy, political tradition and the

revolutionary upheavals of the world. His sympathy for the struggle of the peoples of Latin America for political and social self-determination inspired many of his students to undertake reformist and even revolutionary activity in the Protestant churches of that continent. Thus I found in him a deep understanding of our theological struggle, of the question of the fate of our country, and even of the profound social upheavals then rocking Eastern Europe. So the ground for my theological work at Princeton was prepared, and the establishment of lively contacts with the students facilitated.

I did not experience in America any of the stormy tension which had shaken theology schools there ten and twenty years earlier, the tension between fundamentalism and modernism. The efforts of Reinhold Niebuhr and his colleagues to revise and deepen modern theology had, in my judgment, greatly influenced every area of American Protestantism. Fundamentalism, which had a literalistic understanding of biblical authority and which emphasized certain biblical themes of personal faith and church community, had lost its influence precisely because theological modernism had transformed itself by means of a more responsible study of the Bible.

The American way of life

But I had a very strong feeling that the ecclesiastical and religious life of both American modernists and fundamentalists was far more deeply influenced by rationalism and moralism than was true in Europe. America was born during the period of the Enlightenment and in a Puritan atmosphere. Thus the Christology even of orthodox Protestants was based more on reason and morality, without the ardour of the biblical, prophetic and apostolic message. At the same time, the life of the American churches bore the imprint of the practical mind of

59

the pioneers, with its leaning towards questions of organization. Romanticism, in the European sense of the attempt to penetrate to the depths of the inner man, his emotional turmoil and his related restless spiritual convulsions, was quite foreign to the average American. The romantic passion was replaced by a longing for pioneering adventure on the so-called frontiers of civilized and non-civilized territories. Even that which we call revivalism (emphasis on conversion and regeneration) had an essentially practical meaning in the American context (living without alcohol or tobacco, having a well ordered family life, etc.).

When I arrived in America the influence of Kierkegaard and even—though cautiously—that of Swiss dialectical theology, was beginning to penetrate theological and philosophical thought. Attempts were being made to deepen the exploration of men's spiritual and intellectual life, a task for which rational and conventionally moral ways of thinking were insufficient.

I have said that American history has not known a romantic period. Related to this is an insufficient sense of history. America had enough to do bringing civilization to its great territory, stretching from the Atlantic to the Pacific. It had its small wars with Mexico and Spain, but otherwise it stayed on the fringe of international politics. After the first world war an almost pathological isolationism emerged. The vast majority of Americans was convinced that the entrance of their country into the war had been a mistake. They saw the task of post-war politics as the building of an economic and social life proper to America—the American way of life—and believed that they should have nothing to do with what went on in Europe or any other continent. Economic expansion was conceded, but was not seen as having any relationship to politics. People were convinced that the growing power of the dollar, and its economic and financial penetration into the rest of the world had nothing in common with colonialism, and that there was a fundamental difference between this and the colonial hegemony of the various European nations, especially Great Britain.

At the time of the shattering tensions in Europe (1938–40), it was difficult to convince even thinking Americans that America risked being dragged into the whirlpool which would result in catastrophe and that we should find ourselves on the threshold of a real world revolution. 'Once before we made the mistake of letting ourselves be forced into a world war, and no one will get us into another'—how many times did we hear that line of argument!

Without compass

The fate of Czechoslovakia evoked expressions of genuine sympathy for the Czechoslovak peoples. But few Americans were aware that it was a question of their responsibility. America alone was to blame for the crisis which developed in Europe in that, although one of the victorious powers in 1918, she refused to join the League of Nations; she brought the policies of Woodrow Wilson to a catastrophic end. America simply did not understand the significance of historical events. She did not understand what was going on in Europe, what the revolution of 1917 meant, and that we were then in the midst of a serious crisis for liberal democracy which would affect her as well as Europe.

Today, a quarter of a century later, we understand much better the historical significance of Franklin D. Roosevelt who prudently but conscientiously led the American people to the point that they began to understand their responsibility, not only for themselves but for the whole world. I do not know what the American people would have done if the Japanese had not attacked on December 7, 1941. America entered the war reluctantly, compelled, against her will, by events outside her territory. That is why the great majority of Americans did not grasp the significance of the history of the times; they were led by their practical interests, the consciousness of their own worth and human dignity. So America stood at the end of the war like a man who has lost his compass. She had not come to a deep understanding of her own guilt and shortcomings, nor of her responsibility for the creation of a new international order.

This is why today most Americans do not understand the revolutionary social upheavals taking place all over the world, why they do not understand the movement of history and the necessity of rising above one's own interests, of seeing both the obvious and the hidden relationships among different countries and cultures. This failure, in my judgment, is what has led to such catastrophes as the war in Vietnam. I am of course leaving out many concrete details. What I wish to say is just that the anti-Chinese policy of America, the war in Vietnam, and everything connected with it, stem from a lack of awareness of the significance of history and from the feeling that the American way of life is morally superior.

I hope that these words will not be misinterpreted. How could it ever be forgotten that the United States is also the country of Abraham Lincoln and F. D. Roosevelt? Whoever knows the people of America at close hand, whoever knows them in their private, family and civic lives cannot help having a certain love and admiration for them. There is something direct in them, something spontaneous that is free from the conventions that restrain the peoples of old Europe. We experienced many examples of simple human kindness during our stay in America. But my experiences there had the effect of reinforcing my own understanding of historical reversals and changes. In Europe I was shaken by the current of historical changes and was forced to struggle even in my faith with history itself. In America the lack of any sense of history or comprehension of the great revolutionary events of the previous half-century, convinced me even more firmly that we cannot take a single intelligent political step forward without a real understanding of what is going on in the world.

An almost metaphysical fear

It convinced me that the Church must pay constant attention to the meaning of historical events, to the kind of historical situation in which it is living, so that it can understand man and carry out its work fearlessly even in the most difficult and adverse situations. The Church cannot live in isolation of spirit or in any egotistical feeling of its own dignity and superiority.

This was a useful theological school for me. That which I had lived and thought through during the period between the two wars became much clearer to me during my stay in America. Theology and the Church are called to struggle for man in the deepest depths of his inner life. At the same time, however, they are placed in the midst of the stream of history and the struggle for man in social and political terms. In the event of historical and social upheavals, the Church and theology can be hopelessly confused if they have not penetrated through to an understanding of the very core of their mission and message.

All this became clearer to me during the shocks of the war and its aftermath, as I observed the manner in which theologians and church groups reacted to the problems and tasks of the time. An insufficiently deep grounding in Christology added much to the confusion. Even men like Reinhold Niebuhr who had long been grappling with theological and political questions, became frightened about the future of liberal democratic society in their country, and failed to master theologically the spread of the Soviet Union's socialist revolution into Central Europe.

I thought a great deal about the reasons for this confusion. In so far as I thought realistically, I could understand why certain aspects of what the Soviets had done, both before and after the war, might make even open and socially progressive Western Christians uneasy. But it was imperative to master theologically even the negative and disturbing sides of Soviet socialism and to look courageously and in depth at the changes brought about as a result of the catastrophe of the war. Even the 'Social Gospel' movement, with its much-needed protest against the bourgeois-oriented churches of America, remained content with a moral and rational analysis of the contemporary situation. It lost something of the burning core of the message both of the Apostles and of the Old Testament prophets. Thus it left many of its adherents in great dismay in the atmosphere of the post-war years.

The spirit of American politics changed quickly after the death of F. D. Roosevelt and the old anti-communism, which was dying down somewhat as a result of the hardships the war brought to the Soviet Union, began to reassert itself. The American people wholeheartedly supported the Soviet people so long as they were suffering and in retreat before Hitler's armies. But from the moment when things began to change, in early 1943, when the Red Army began its unchecked march to the German borders, an almost metaphysical fear of the 'communist menace' grew up.

The Man of Sorrows

It was not easy for American Christians to grasp that the changes confronting us were not just political or governmental changes in the balance of power—that we were standing at a cross-roads of history. The idea that mankind would develop and evolve according to the models of West European and American democracy was shattered. So was the wishful belief, which had been current in church circles, that the whole world would be evangelized in the course of the present generation. What disturbed Westerners was not just that their political and economic system was at stake. They were uneasy because certain elements of their existential *Weltanschauung* had come under the judgment of history.

I mentioned above that the average American did not take on himself his share of responsibility for the international crisis of the inter-war years, that he lived in an aura of superiority *vis à vis* the political confusion of Europe. Thus he did not go through any sort of serious self-examination or see his own mistakes and shortcomings. Moreover, he was almost offended by the emergence on the stage of history of a nation which until only a short time before had been ignored and which professed a totally different concept of socio-political organization and future development. Moreover, this was a nation which officially professed atheism, and its appearance raised questions about the very existence of the Christian Church and Christian society. This situation called for deep self-examination; it was necessary to ask how the world war had produced such an outcome, what was the meaning and significance of atheistic culture, and how one could wrestle spiritually with this new situation. American reaction had an easy task not only in initiating, but—with its systematic propaganda—in hardening and developing the cold war. Even progressive theologians did everything possible, during this period, to convince their churches and public opinion that their criticism of certain aspects of America had nothing to do with communism and even lent support to the struggle against communism.

The whole immense problem of modern democracy and communism, of the historical changes which followed the second world war, and of the international organization of modern man acrose before us like an onslaught against the very foundations of our theology and our efforts to penetrate to the core of the Gospel, to the essence of God's action in the Old and New Covenants. What was involved was a descent to the furthest depths of man's corruption and confusion, to the point where the crucified Jesus of Nazareth began his struggle for man's salvation and freedom. It also involved the fact that this defenceless Man of Sorrows has become the Lord of history, the Lord of a mankind disoriented by the war, and Lord of the future.

A challenge to the churches

The future of world society will be different from that envisaged by the average American, naïve and self-satisfied as he is. Communism is something different from the pictures by which West Europeans and then Americans caricatured and demonized it. The victory of the Soviet Union was not a misfortune but rather the result of unbearable social and political relations within European society. This victory is no threat to modern democracies; rather it is a call to them to improve their social order, to nourish it and strengthen it by social reconstruction. The atheism of Eastern Europe is a challenge to the Christian churches, asking them whether they really believe the Gospel and follow in the footsteps of Jesus of Nazareth, or whether they are using the faith to cover up the political and economic interests of financial groups or perhaps to provide cultural values, no doubt precious but also precarious.

It is true that the people of the Soviet Union have gone through several moral and political deformations in the process of building their communism. It is also true that after the war Soviet society lived in an atmosphere often marked and full of fear. It was necessary to give the exhausted and war-crippled Soviet society lived in an atmosphere often morbid and full country and in creating a new world order. But American politics for a whole decade nourished an almost metaphysical anti-Soviet fear and for several years gave rein to dark longings, and occasionally even active hopes that the threat of 'communist aggression and tyranny' might be eliminated, either by external pressures or as the result of a new catastrophe. Self-righteousness and fear dominated the Western world, under the leadership of America, and made the struggle for spiritual freedom, for the freedom of faith, and for the creative mission of the Church theologically very difficult.

Neither theology nor the Church was ready for the profound changes that took place in political and international order. They did not see what was at the root of the crisis through which men and society were going. Fundamentalism (an ossified cult of biblical texts) became a cover for, and instrument of, self-righteousness and for reactionary politics on both internal and international levels. Modernistic theology came to the defence of liberal democracy and the so-called 'open society', an attitude that was more negative than creative. What was necessary was a penetrating examination of the roots of communism in the spiritual, cultural, political and social history of Russia. It was necessary to analyse the extent to which the isolation of East Europe may have been a cause of the second world war and of some of the negative aspects of Soviet society, and to ask oneself on what positive values and hopes, which Western man might have in entering into contact with East Europe, one might lean for support in building a new international order. The cold war, to which all classes and groups in Western society succumbed, from left to right, caused irreparable damage to all of us, damage not only in the political and economic respect, but in the very structure of our spiritual life.

SECULARIZATION: OPPORTUNITY AND THREAT FOR MANKIND

The varnish of religiosity

All this leads me to one more remark. America stands at the forefront of the forces of secularization. The scientific management of society, technological progress, highly refined organizational methods with all their advantages (cybernetics and the ingenious methods of what is called managerialism), and the almost feverish efforts devoted to developing consumer society—all of these had already reached unprecedented levels even by the end of the war and the early post-war years. It is a process that cannot be stopped and which is now making itself felt in the life of every country of the world.

Immediately after the war church life acquired the aura of something fashionable. Americans began to believe, at least subconsciously, that atheistic communism must be countered with a society built on Christian traditions and bustling church activity. In fact, however, beneath this varnish of religiosity, and even under the varnish of fundamentalism, a radically secular style of life was taking shape. The war had brought increased wealth to North America and with the fall of Europe's various colonial empires, the United States became the economic and financial sovereign of almost the whole world. Many areas of American life still present problems—the question of racism, for example, or the millions who live on the fringes of society at a level of income below the minimum needed for a normal life. This rich, well-armed nation living in superabundance, has taken its personal and social life into its own hands and, in spite of all formal religiosity, has relegated God to second or third place.

The goals towards which the human race is aiming itself today have been unfolded in American life, to a hitherto unimaginable extent. Even in American theology there have been and still are voices, similar to those heard in another context in Europe, proclaiming that secularization must be recognized not as negative but as a positive force and, to a certain extent, a result of the biblical message itself. The Gospel has demythologized life and the world. It has swept away all idols and demons, with all the altars erected in their honour. The Gospel has made the world the world, man what he is. In this sense it has freed man from all superstitions and religious taboos, and from all tendencies to mix the Godhead with the methods of human intervention. All this is true. I would want to say in this connection that I can go at least part of the way with those theologians who talk of the death of God. I can go with them so long as it is clear that the God whom they condemn to death is a creature of human thought, speculation and superstitious self-intoxication. I also understand the protest of those who reject cheap complaints of the Church against secularization and disagree with the opinion that it is in itself a falling away from God.

Man come of age

But saying this does not solve the problem. Even a secularized world has its dangers. A technically advanced, economically mature, scientifically developed nation (or even individual) eventually, by the force of inner necessity, reaches existential questions, problems and tasks which the civilized means of science or technology cannot solve. Mass media of culture, science and technology, and the organized manipulation of men's lives may all cripple man. At home and at work people become the victims of that which they have created. The dangers to civilized humanity, to human inter-relations between countries and races, and between rich and poor, have never been as great as they are today. In what lies the germ of the decomposition of civilized man and humanity? And how can we help the man of today to deal with his inner and outer suffering?

I have no desire to look contemptuously on, or piously to bewail a secularized (and hence, it is said, godless) world. But my experiences in America forced me to think seriously about the biblical account of the tower of Babel and about the weariness of the advanced and well organized world into which the prophets and the apostles brought the Gospel.

Of course, this is not just a question for America. It is a question for all of us, regardless of the political or cultural area we live in. Modern man has come of age through scientific technological and cultural efforts. The best representatives of American theology accepted these theses of Bonhoeffer as their own. But maturity is not the same as wisdom or self-discipline. Man come of age cannot go back to his childhood; he has more serious spiritual breaches, conflicts and maladies than has a child. And there is still the question of how to help him, of what kind of medicine he needs. Clearly the old methods of church or missionary work will not help. This man with his science, technology and civilization must be positively understood. But this very man is walking above the abyss between life and death. This man faces the danger that he may annihilate himself and the possibility that his confidence in himself may deprive him of the finest and deepest roots of real humanity.

FOUR

On the Ruins of the Second World War

After 1947

AND SO WE COME TO my final remarks about my theological and ecclesiastical struggles.

ACCOUNT OF MY STAY IN AMERICA

As if on a balcony

I remained for a short time after the second world war at my theological post at Princeton. Gradually I came to the end of my engagements, and no longer accepted new ones. Twice I made short visits to Czechoslovakia, in 1945 and again the next year, to determine whether I would return to my old post and whether I would be accorded the confidence which is indispensable to a theologian or preacher. Six years is a long time. But the years which I spent away from my country had brought a deep, almost cataclysmic turning point in the history of the whole world, in the history of all Europe, and of course in the history of our people and churches in Czechoslovakia. In America I was able to live through the pre-war, wartime and post-war periods of the American people, to see how America's isolation changed through participation in the international military struggle and in her post-war fear of her ally and principal co-victor, the Soviet Union. I observed the fall of the old power, the beginning of the end of the colonial system, and the first attempts at co-operation in the United Nations. But I lived as if on a balcony: observing, registering and all the while passionately living through the conflagration with all its horrors and its eventually victorious end. Our people were living at the time under the tyranny of Hitler, in great personal and national danger, mutilated, suppressed but for that very reason inspired to ever new resistance. The difference between my situation and that of my brother and sister citizens was bound to leave deep traces in our ways of thinking, in our emotions, and in our views of the present and the future of human society. Several of my close friends and colleagues had died on the gallows or in concentration camps. These were questions of differing existential experiences which had to be solved.

With a certain anxiety, I returned and began to explore the atmosphere and take the pulse of my native land and church. I was by no means sure that I would be accepted with confidence or openness. In particular, I did not know whether I would understand what had taken place at home, whether I should discover a real contact with people who had in the interval lived through such great dangers, accompanied, for many of them, by great suffering. Many of my American friends tried to convince me that my place was to stay in America. But for me there was no other way than that of returning to Czechoslovakia.

The American theologian

I look back on my life at Princeton and on my colleagues and students with pleasure and gratitude. And I feel that by staying in America I enlarged my horizons and was better able to test the theological interpretations to which I had become accustomed in Europe. I was forced in the case of every biblical, theological or dogmatic concept to search for a way to make it understandable to American students. Theological problems which had been part of my life at home before the war and which grew out of the biblical message, the Reformation, and such modern thought as that of Kierkegaard, Dostoevsky, Karl Barth and L. Ragaz were totally foreign to the average American student. I had to orient myself towards the American way of thinking and the corresponding spiritual and ecclesiastical structures.

The American Christian, with his practical outlook and dislike of the problematic way of thinking, finds it difficult to understand that in essence we begin to understand the Gospel only when we move on the frontiers of human life, face to face with that which goes beyond normal intellectual, ethical or political categories. An American theologian asks of every biblical sentence or dogmatic thesis: What does this mean in practice for me? Often there is a great deal of naïveté and, as it were, an elementary character in this. But it is a great help to theologians to ask this question during their expositions. I understand that even theology, in the very core of its thinking, takes on a scientific exactness when it confronts its theses with the concrete life of the world and the Church, and when it discerns the practical content of its opinions. It is not the same as the pragmatism of William James who otherwise well interprets the structure of American thinking, of American politics, and of the ecclesiastical atmosphere in the United States. It is not a question of measuring theological or philosophical truth by practical efficacy. The efficacy of practical activity lasts but a short time or is only illusory. The Gospel of the Cross warns us against such cheap pragmatism. What is involved is understanding that the message of the Bible intervenes in the life of nations and of persons with consequences which are not immediately perceived but which constitute an urgent call for self-knowledge and practical decision both for the individual and for the church community. 'By their fruits ye shall know them' remains a painful check on theological activity, even on our interpretations of the prophets and the Gospel.

I write about this because my stay in America was not only a temporary asylum for me, but also a useful theological school. But if I feel myself tempted to pass a severe judgment on certain phenomena of American mentality and politics, this does not mean that I will ever forget all that I gained, spiritually and intellectually, from my stay in America. Even if I did not hesitate in my decision to return home, I still left Princeton enriched and indeed, with a deepened faith.

CZECHOSLOVAKIA AFTER THE WAR

God in the depths

Two short books I wrote while at Princeton are evidence of the two fundamental questions which dominated my spiritual life. I became aware of the fact that the whole structure of civilization to which we have become accustomed in the West had been shattered to its very foundations. Western man had been ennervated by his scepticism about the values of his civilization and its future hopes. Thus the use of the word 'Doom', meaning fall, in the title of my book, *Doom and Resurrection*. But when we look into the depths of our own crisis and take it as a matter of life and death, we see a gleam of hope and the near-presence of a life-giving source. At the same time I thought of the legacy of my friend and collaborator from inter-war days, Emmanuel Radl (who died in 1942). I probed the roots of his thinking in the life of our country, of

75

his struggle both with the significant and the decadent phenomena in the independent state which was Czechoslovakia,
and of his spiritual strivings and efforts to improve things
human. I wrote a book, *The Don Quixote of Czech Philosophy*,
about him. I published my occasional comments on international affairs and the catastrophes of the war with Otakar
Odlozilik in the book *From the Other Shore*.

Thus the circle of my theological and political struggles
closed in around me: the crisis of civilization, the legacy of the
creative history of my people, the attempt to understand what
was going on in the tempestuous history of the period and the
sort of commitments which might be waiting for us after the
war. But throughout all this I was constantly thinking about
what the Gospel of the Old and New Covenant might have
to offer to the depths of the human heart, and to the life of the
Church and in the historical struggles of the time. It was my
strong impression that American Christians and even theologians lacked a real existential passion for the very core of
Christology, for the descent to the depths through which God
in his sovereign love and mercy leads the liberating struggle
against the corruption, impotence and mortality of mankind.
Of course I asked myself whether we did not suffer the same
lack. Will Europeans see on the ruins of the old world and
amidst the tombs of the fifty million who perished during the
war the figure of Jesus of Nazareth; will they hear his painful
question: 'Why have you forsaken me?'

I hope that these comments will not be thought of as
theological theories more or less doctrinaire in character or as
a sentimental last gasp. What I am concerned with here are
the questions which preoccupied me existentially towards the
end of my stay in America and the time of my return home.

In the Soviet orbit

I returned in 1947, at a time when Europe was still living amid ruins, but when it still seemed that the victors were going to reach agreement on the reorganization of the continent and the establishment of an international order. Czechoslovakia became part of the area under the direct influence of the Soviet Union. The whole atmosphere was marked by this fact. But many people did not take it seriously. During my two visits from America (1945–46) I encountered many who declared that this was but a transitional stage for Central Europe and that sooner or later it would be possible to return to things as they had been in the days before Munich, that is to say, to take up things where we had left off towards the end of 1938. It disturbed me that particularly in our church community there were few people who had really examined the cataclysmic changes wrought by the world-wide catastrophe, and who were aware that it would be necessary to work out a new order.

Our bonds with Eastern Europe, that is to say with the Soviet Union, seemed to me the inescapable outcome of pre-war errors, of the devastations of the war and the goals of social revolution embodied in the Soviet Union. The sufferings of the Soviet people during the war were indescribable. Their sacrifices were without number. Their memories of having been excluded from international affairs between the two wars could not be forgotten. Their responsibility in building the new order rested on the victory for which they had paid in blood. The Soviet Union was forced into the war and its advance to the Elbe was the result not of aggressive tendencies to domination, but rather of its life and death struggle. Moreover, it was impossible to forget that at the time of their most serious crisis the Czechoslovak people were abandoned by the Western powers and delivered into the hands of Nazi

Germany. It was not possible to vouch for Czeckoslovakia's security or even for its future existence as a nation without leaning on the support of a country that would assume the role which the Western states rejected in 1938.

At the same time, however, it was clear to every careful observer of the wartime and post-war events that the societies of the future would undergo profound social changes, and that Soviet socialism would become one of the models of social change and in a measure which could not be overlooked in history.

The tasks before us

Armed with these convictions, I returned home. It was clear to me that complex psychological and cultural hardships were going to be part of all this. The Czechoslovak people had grown up for centuries in the context of Central European and Western cultural traditions. Catholicism and Protestantism bound them to the West. The spiritual structure of our people differs from the Russian mentality, whether conservative or socialist. I also knew that the communists, who took over the leadership of the state and society, were not going to be sufficiently prepared for the difficult tasks that awaited them. They were not going to have enough specialists to direct economic life, administration and education. Our socialism would carry the mark of Soviet socialism because that of Western and Central Europe (Germany, France, Austria and Britain) had not accomplished its mission in the inter-war period. All this placed us very much at a watershed in our history, and set for us immense political, economic and even human tasks.

Even so, however, there was, as far as I could see, no other way than to accept this situation positively, to understand it as the outcome of the upheavals in the very structure of European history. These were not just political changes; they were part of the development of history. It was the roots of our way of living that had changed. I repeat, even we Protestants were not prepared inwardly or armed for such a revolution. The First Republic of Czechoslovakia had conformed to our political ideals, our desires and our whole cultural mood. The political and ideological programme of the Socialist Republic went beyond the context of our conceptions and even our intellectual powers.

Under the old Austro-Hungarian monarchy, Czech Protestants had been at the forefront of political progress. In the First Republic they were displaced from this position by the socialist currents at play in the new state. Even so, they considered themselves to be protagonists of Masaryk's democratic humanism. After 1945, even more after February, 1948, when the communists seized power in Czechoslovakia, they found themselves politically, socially and culturally outside the mainstream of those groups which were building the socialist state. It was not easy to come to terms with this fact. In my opinion, the socio-political degradation of a large majority of Czech Protestants was largely responsible for their distrustful and often even hostile attitudes towards the communist structure of civil life. The atheist ideology, often vulgarized and intellectually and spiritually superficial, reinforced the distaste and reluctance of Czech Protestants. What was needed was an extraordinarily penetrating view of the historical changes of the preceding fifty years so that we might understand that we had to begin where we were placed by the upheaval of February, 1948.

The point of meeting

It was essential to have a positive understanding of the efforts required by the Soviet people to ensure the security of their western frontiers. We stood at the border line and had to serve at a point where post-war East and West Europe met. We are a Western-oriented country and we cannot give up great treasures of our history. At the same time, however, we are called upon, by our language and our affinities with the literary and spiritual history of the Russian people creatively to unite, there on the frontier, the genuine goals of Western democracy with the social and socialist import of the Russian cultural and religious traditions. But it was of course also necessary to struggle for a creative role for the Church of Jesus Christ, which, with total freedom, enters into a new society to fulfil its mission of faith, service and hopeful expectation. We had to combat in ourselves the feelings of despondency, fatalism and helplessness which so dangerously gnawed at our church life and even more at our faith that the future was in the hands of one who had called us to service. Many of our Christians fell to the fatalistic fancy that sooner or later communism, by its own decision, its tactics, and its goals, would suppress the Church and bury it in the ground.

THE DANGER OF A GHETTO

An artificial dike

But it was this point that I was beset by a pressing question. Where is it written that the communists would be the sole masters of our future? We talked, in the Church, of Jesus Christ as Lord, and in theology we had often, almost too much, emphasized the so-called eschatological aspects of the Christian faith, especially in our reading of the Bible—and all at once all this somehow lost its living strength for us, its spiritual fervour and its power to convince. How sterile theological doctrine can sometimes be, and how even a beautiful church tradition grows cold!

Theologians and preachers have forgotten that it is their responsibility to take up the never-ending struggle—a struggle indeed—positive and critical—for a new reality. A large part of the faithful retired into their churches and prayers, and felt themselves to be strangers to public life, whether political and social, or economic and cultural. Again it was necessary to ask: What is the meaning of socialism and of communism. What is the meaning of democracy? Is it not necessary to give to humanitarian ideals, previously thought of as uniquely political, a positive social content which would enable them to be understood by those who—despite their immaturity and lack of preparation—have taken on the administration of our villages, towns, regions and the state itself? If we shut ourselves up in our churches, if we hide—as it was said—in a ghetto, in closed circles, will we not go into an intellectual decline? The life of thought and our moral life—will not they wither away, and our responsibility fade for those who are called by history to carry the heavy burdens of political and social duty? The danger is great when our faith in the Gospel weakens and rots, and becomes just a personal consolation and a cloak of self-righteous respectability. Such a faith would be a flight or at most an artificial dike against the winds and tempests of the new historical situation. Yes, there even were instances where people fled to the churches as a protest against the new society. What a retreat from the battleground! Faith in the Gospel cannot be reduced to mere spiritual consolation, to religious feelings and to a frame of mind which flees from the world. The Gospel is a continuous struggle for man and society, for his body and his soul, for the mastering of the serious and burdensome questions of public as well as personal life. Thus it was necessary, I repeat, for believing members of our congregations to take the historical shocks seriously and not to consider them as temporary inconveniences and to keep on looking backwards.

QUESTIONS ABOUT ATHEISM

Question without answer

A second task is connected with this one. Is genuine communist socialism existentially, i.e. essentially, atheistic? Is the opposition to the Church and religion which we see among communists a permanent assault against the essential core of the Gospel, against the God of the Old and New Covenants, against the Church in its genuine character of love, sacrifice and an unselfish struggle for man? Nearly all the replies to these questions, as much from the communist as the Christian side, seemed to me to be positive. Yes, to be a communist means to be an unconditional atheist. Communist society will necessarily be atheistic. Few communists or Christians knew how to look beneath the surface of daily life or to keep themselves from being disoriented by the atmosphere of progaganda, vulgar atheism, or ecclesiastical prejudices about the impossibility of serious dialogue with communists. One cannot understand the question in depth unless one goes back to the origins of the socialist movement and its efforts to construct from the old society one which is more just and, in a word, more humane. There were not many people who were anxious to learn that human life and history are much more complex than they are understood to be by nominal, conventional Christians or by communists who are too often sustained by propaganda or so influenced by environment that they lose all critical faculty. The socialist movement and the communist campaign over the last hundred and fifty years have encountered churches bound by their organization to the old society, whether feudal or, later, bourgeois. Atheist propaganda against the Church did not develop out of a denial of God and his work, or from a denial of the Gospel and its spiritual power. It grew rather from an opposition to the Church as a definite socio-political form which in the name of a so-called religion, defended the old social order with all its injustices, its cultural backwardness, and its conservative immobility. Moreover, the communists in their atheistic ideology, do not themselves make much effort to understand the real significance and basis of their attitude towards religion and the churches.

Were we right in affirming that communism is not essentially atheistic? This is a question which cannot be answered today because nobody is in a position to answer it. It is a question over which it is necessary to struggle intellectually and ethically, at the very depths of human thought, of the human heart and conscience. It is a question which can be answered only in the process of history. And here what matters is whether a Christian in the purity of his faith and his understanding of man joins the struggle and demonstrates by the audacity of his faith, by his love for his neighbour, and his optimism about the future, that he is not just the passive object of history or even of the new society, but rather the co-author and co-architect of the new order.

My 'betrayal' of the Church

The spiritual situation of the world, especially in those societies hitherto nominally Christian, shows that not just the communist, but all modern men are conditioned by an atheistic atmosphere and that the evolution of science and technology is a permanent assault on the traditional structure of the Church and everything we call religion. This we must always remember. But at the same time we must ruthlessly examine ourselves, to see whether communism and modern science and technology in general do not challenge, and rightly so, our idols and fetishes, our superstition and backwardness, and our lazy attitude to the real events taking place in our society.

The new historical situation in our country confronted us with complex intellectual and ethical questions. It was not a question primarily of protecting the activities of the Church, but rather of understanding man in his inner and social life, of seeking new ways and means of thinking and even new words for describing our tasks. We were forced (and we still are) to control ourselves, to know ourselves in all our weaknesses as well as in our real tasks. In particular, it was a question of undertaking our work with a deeper understanding of the Gospel, with genuine joy, without fear or deadening fatalism.

To present our task to Christians, simply, comprehensibly and urgently, was not easy. There were many mistakes, small and large. Often those who least deserved the distrust and suspicion of the new leaders of our society were weeded out. This often happened in the countryside or in smaller towns where people or families settled private scores under the guise of politics. I was not happy when people walked about with gloomy faces and spread around them a peevish, gloomy atmosphere. But it was important that even these people be understood seriously and fairly, although, from a world view and in a historical context, they were wrong. It was a difficult pastoral task: to avoid confirming people in their false political opinions and old social (and class) interests, and still to have compassion for their personal or family sufferings, and an understanding of their ethical or political disagreement with many essential or incidental aspects of the new society. And to help those who needed it.

When I look back on the time around 1948, I constantly and self-critically ask myself whether I have found the right words to express all that has taken place and to deal with people's personal experiences. So much bitterness and sometimes even malice was in people's hearts—as was shown by innumerable anonymous letters. They came; frequently they threatened severe punishment for my 'betrayal' of our church and of the Gospel itself. Of course, I must also say that in these critical times there were many fine people in my church, in the smaller communities, and, yes, even among Catholics, who were a great support to me, although they may not have been right in the thick of the public and church struggle.

HISTORY DOES NOT STAND STILL EITHER FOR CHRISTIANS OR FOR COMMUNISTS

The beginning of the dialogue

Readers will forgive me if in this connection I mention again the importance of historical perspective. History cannot retrace its steps; 1938 cannot repeat itself. The very structure of Europe, of the whole world, was changed and we had to start from that naked, brutal, but also hopeful fact. History does not stand still. Certain changes furnish a permanent basis for future development. One should be on one's guard against those who would like to turn back the wheel of history and obliterate the results of wartime upheavals. Individuals and churches, political parties and nations must be admonished to accept in a penitent spirit what the end of the war has brought about. On the other hand, it is important that Christians and communists, who have retained some freshness of thinking and are capable of love and hope, should together prepare for the morrow, for its spiritual and political content will depend on our responsible co-operation. History has not ended either for Christians or for communists.

We were not prepared, after 1948, for dialogue with our communist friends on political and spiritual questions. The communists had been through a long period of narrow dogmatism. Psychologically and sociologically, this may have been a necessary transition from the revolutionary shocks, from the uncertainty about the structure of the new order. But that period should not last too long. In particular, it required of us a daring and creative responsibility and co-operation. The Church should not be paralysed by fear and by desire to protect itself from the world. On their side, the communists could not fail to give evidence of their poverty of intellectual and spiritual freshness, of political wisdom and human foresight. A country can be governed by suppression and authoritarian rule—but only for a short time. Equally it is also only for a short time that the Church can take shelter from the storm, waiting for the weather to clear. This situation should have led both us and the communists to think seriously about our faith and convictions. Without ardent, enthusiastic hearts, without the passion of conviction, without a courageous view of the morrow, nothing great can be built. Thus I came to have more and more regard for genuine, committed communists, and at the same time a strong aversion for those who, lacking personal conviction and disinterested self-sacrifice, bungled over communism and the future by their hardness and arrogance.

I welcomed it when committed communists tried to win Christians to their side. And I know that many sincere communists, step by step, were prepared to take sincere Christians seriously and to think about what they had to contribute to society. Sincere Christians and communists understood that the future had set us the most difficult of tasks and human questions. We all had to free ourselves from mistrust, doctrinal prejudices and especially fear. We Christians were afraid of communists and they of us. We did not know where to begin our dialogue and co-operation.

The fear of disenchantment

At the beginning of February, 1948, just before our socialist revolution, we gathered at the Philosophy Department of Charles University and tried to understand and convince each other. I no longer remember all the details, but I still recall the basic theme because I have never abandoned it. It was: As a Christian theologian I have nothing against socialism. Even from a religious viewpoint it is much closer to me than is bourgeois liberal democracy. I am ready to help in the construction of a socialist society. But I warned that the fundamental problems of socialist man would still weigh heavily upon us, even after our society has been politically, socially and economically rebuilt. The basic human problems remain whatever the structure of society. This is not to diminish the value of socialist reconstruction. It is just recognition of a fact—that man cannot be manipulated even in a socialist society, that some questions will always remain, questions of guilt and punishment of conscience and responsibility, of pain and suffering, of death and destruction. Only after the new society has been formed will it be clear how man as such transcends scientific categories and technical means, and how not even a perfect social order can satisfy man as such. What shall we do then? Will not you communists be forced to listen to us and to

87

seek help from us? And are we Christians not obliged to think about what we have to offer to men today, who, in spite of all they have gained from science, technology and social revolution, still find themselves confronted, in the new society, with their old human problems, sufferings and unfulfilled hopes?

Critical questions were aimed at both sides, at communists and committed Christians. I was not sure that Christians, individually or as churches, were sufficiently prepared for or equal to the task which had been assigned to them. Several of the Marxists who were present thought that my opinions reflected an outmoded pessimism that had nothing to do with the new society. We parted amicably, but in disagreement over our view of history, and of man and his mission. And we parted for what was to become a long time.

I mention this discussion of ours because, in the light of the last twenty years, we can better understand the anxious questions we raised then and compare today's atmosphere with that of the last days before the radical upheaval of our social order. My reaction to the communists' hope that the social order could change men and gradually solve all their personal and social questions was rather more positive than negative. I have long preferred people who believe in something, who fight for something, and who have thought out plans for the future. Scepticism and cynicism have always been foreign to me; they run counter to my views of man and the future. Nonetheless, I was deeply concerned over the naïve hope that science, technology, the structure of society and its atmosphere could change people as such for the better. I was afraid that this naïveté (as well as abstract notions about the future) might give birth to a disenchantment that could result in an unfortunate and socially destructive cynicism. Perhaps as a theologian and former pastor my eyes were open to the way in which people cling, within the Church, to much that is unjust, irresponsible, and secretly selfish. I could easily imagine what moral testing the citizens of the new socialist society would have to endure and how the lack of truthfulness and responsibility would remain one of the greatest obstacles to the construction of an equitable socialist order.

We could not go back

We felt this very strongly in the years immediately following February, 1948. Not every communist was adequate to his party, political and educational tasks. Alongside the self-sacrificing and enthusiastic workers in the Communist Party, in the government, and in the communes were many careerists and opportunists, for whom it was enough just to paint everything red, who pursued their own interests, though under new symbols and in new guises. There were many who sought to feather their own nests. To this was added a kind of demonic plague of suspicion and mistrust which lay heavy on society. We all know about the injustices and bloody personal sacrifices which went on within the party and the government. The results began to show up very soon: people became sceptical and irresponsible in their attitudes towards their duties as citizens and towards their work. We became aware of the fact that a socialist society cannot be built without a dedicated attitude to one's work, without personal commitment, and without relationships of real friendship towards the people.

Very soon it became necessary to appeal to people in terms of so-called material interest—to make them realize that their wages, or their personal interest, was at stake, and that the only way to ensure them was through work. A kind of moral vacuum followed the changes of 1948, both in personal life and in the attitudes towards work. The appeal to material interest was a necessary, but disturbing element in socialist education. The old authorities and moral norms were not replaced by norms or authorities capable of evoking commitment and ethical intensivity, as intellectual and educational prudence would have suggested; they just fell by the way-side. But we also found ourselves in a situation in which it was necessary to struggle, responsibly and with an understanding of the challenges of the moment, against the inner barriers to social progress. We could not go back. By the end of the 'fifties the structure of the socialist states had been consolidated. Not even those most opposed to socialism still believed that it would be possible, by force or by secret infiltration, to liquidate the new socio-political order. But for that very reason we faced a complex question of what to do in order that the individual might become a convinced and responsible partner in the building of the new society; that he might bring to it everything from our own history and from that of the rest of the world which had helped to raise the level, the dignity, and the freedom of human life.

The heart-beat of a people

I have already said that Russian communism cannot be explained solely by the theory of Marxism or the work of Lenin, that it is necessary to go back, with care and understanding, to its roots in the progressive tendencies of the nineteenth century, as well as in those intellectual movements which cannot really be called progressive. The dialectic of history is complex and is not governed by ephemeral labels such as 'progressive' or 'reactionary'. Poets and writers, often even saints and theologians, can detect motives, tendencies and aspirations in men's personal struggles and in human relationships which go beyond our political or social categories. As we have already said, Merejkovsky called Dostoevsky the prophet of the Russian Revolution. He did not mean just that Dostoevsky had a keen ear for the underground upheavals, and that he led man to the frontiers of faith and doubt, obedience and rebellion, self-sacrificing love and blind obedience. He meant that Dostoevsky, a political conservative, had sensed the rottenness of the old society and the coming of violent storms. All the vulgar slogans about faith and doubt, atheism and godlessness had failed to grasp what was really going on in the mind of a revolutionary accustomed to scientific thinking, technologically mature and ideologically convinced. The conservative Dostoevsky announced the fall of the old pillars of society. But the committed and active revolutionary will soon grasp the complexity of his task. When, after years of construction, he looks at the citizens of the new society, when he gets close enough to hear the very breathing and heartbeats of real people, their conflicts and their sufferings, their deceptions and his own emotional upheaval as the history of his own country and of the whole world reveals the sterility and emptiness of so many of the slogans and high-sounding theories —then there comes a moment when he begins to understand that socialist society is not a workshop for automatons, but that it demands a much deeper understanding of man, history and social progress than he had previously thought.

The modern atmosphere of scepticism and apathy represents a special threat to both communism and Christianity. The committed communist thinks more responsibly and seriously about the problems of man and society than does someone who has no commitment, who is wallowing in scepticism and often even cynicism. As I have said, even in communist society, nothing is more destructive than the scepticism of those who have lost all their illusions and are foundering with no real goals or commitment.

All in the same boat

The realities of the historical situation, the crises of society, the economic failures, and even the weakness of many intellectuals forced us, both Christians and Marxists, to think together about man, about his calling and his future. Communist intellectuals probably understand the critical situation of man today, caught up in the wake of revolutionary events, more intensively than the majority of those Christians who live behind the walls of their churches and temples, following inherited traditions and customs, without seeking to reach an understanding of the life of modern man, what he needs, and what the Church of Christ can give him. This is why I never cease to search my conscience, asking myself if what we have done, if our thinking, our sense of solidarity, our love, and our hope in the future were strong enough to overcome the human crisis that has, to be sure, existed throughout history but which today has taken on particularly shattering dimensions.

I do not like using the vocabulary of religion, especially where questions as real and concrete as those we encounter in contemporary society are concerned. But I spend a great deal of time thinking about how we can really help our neighbours and brothers, regardless of whether or not they are believers or church members, in their struggles and problems, in their hopes and disappointments.

In particular, how does one speak today to young people who have passed through so many different experiences and who are particularly exposed not only to profound confusion, but also to the paralysing atmopshere of apathy and cynicism? How do we speak to them so that they will understand us, so that our words will resound with conviction, so that we are afflicted where they are afflicted, weak where they are weak, and yet still be for them a helping hand and a light on the way, without falling into cheap spiritual self-righteousness? This is a question which concerns the whole world, not just socialist societies. It may even be that in nominally Christian countries, where the Church still has its old prestige, the atmosphere is worse than it is here. Our friends in non-socialist countries might do well to remember that more than once in history the first have been last and the last first. We are all in the same boat, and together we bear the burdens of faithlessness. The crisis of contemporary civilization, and the catastrophic atmosphere of international politics lie heavily on the shoulders of us all.

WHAT IS SACRED FOR MAN?

A love as ardent . . .

One question constantly pursues me: Is there anything genuinely and unconditionally sacred in the life of contemporary man, something before which he can kneel, which can help him to recognize the boundary between what is and what is not permissible? There are many gods and idols set up by people in response to their needs and spiritual presuppositions. Many have been erected in modern society, idols which have led sooner or later to tyranny, brutality and eventually to catastrophe. Modern man, in spite of his scepticism and lack of faith, is always looking for new altars where, under the pressure of society and of administrative regulations, he can kneel as a slave at the very moment when his religious scepticism is most corrosive. In discussing what is sacred, I am thinking about what applies unconditionally and yet liberates man in the depths of his soul—about that which not only liberates, but—even more—enflames him to genuine love towards all who live beside him and for whom, in the depths of his free consciousness, he is responsible.

I am not talking here about some doctrine or new cult, but simply about that which applies to every true disciple of Jesus Christ. I am talking about that real but intangible reflection of the presence of Christ. I cannot find the right words to express what I mean. But believers who withdraw within themselves, and within their churches, and who live in an attitude of some sort of spiritual superiority or even pride, represent to me the 'salt which has lost its savour'. On the other hand, those who believe in the Gospel and who go into this world as if with empty hands, possessing nothing and not thinking highly of themselves, can—so to speak—awaken in people the awareness that this world, confused and imperfect as it is, yet on the way to a better order, has at its heart an altar of holiness where men of liberty and love can kneel, so that, strengthened and enriched, they can go out and share that which has been given them, without thought of recognition or reward.

What I have just said about what is sacred indicates what I mean. The French communist Roger Garaudy recalled, in a discussion on relations between Marxism and Christianity, that not even a Marxist can ignore what saints like Teresa of Avila or John of the Cross have contributed to human life and even to the modern world. What he sought to show was that no external political, social or economic conditions by themselves can ever create such ardent love, self-sacrifice and holy enthusiasm. We could add to the list of names those of many others since the times of the Apostle Paul, from Francis of Assisi, through our Unity of Brethren, innumerable outstanding Anabaptists, and representatives of the Lutheran and Calvinist Reformations, up to the Salvation Army of William

Booth. That which inspired these men was not the rigour of church discipline or orthodoxy: they reached out to Jesus, the Man of Sorrows, who personified absolute holiness to the point of identifying himself with lepers and the poor, with the faithless and the lost, who went through the hell of desolation, and who conquered.

It seems to me that these, the most profound depths of Christology are somehow forgotten or at least put on one side in modern theological circles. Has not the essence of the legacy of the Old Testament, with its prophets and psalms, its exposition of the way of salvation from Abraham to the New Testament, been forgotten? (Is there not a lack here for which Bultmann, Tillich and their followers are responsible?) The Old Testament liberates by its message about holy Israel and its lasting reminder that the pilgrimage from Egypt through the Sinai desert to the Promised Land was a pilgrimage guided by the compassion of the Holy One. Moses and Jeremiah, to name but two, are the prefiguration of what was fulfilled in Jesus of Nazareth. It is in no way a road from below to above, but rather a road from the heights of holy love to the shadows of human impotence. But it is a road that has at its end the promise of a glorious victory (Isaiah 63.7–9). What is it, then, which gives life to the world?

The Creator Spirit

The dialogues into which the historical situation has led us have rendered, and continue to render a great service to our theology. And they force us radically to revise our ways of thinking and our approach to people both in personal contacts and in public activity. Our dialogues, I repeat, are not non-committal theoretical exercises; they are not just on an intellectual level. They require personal involvement and human contact in which abstract logic sometimes loses its force and a spiritual sense and understanding become decisive, an understanding of man, of his words and decisions, of his deepest motives, and of what we call his conscience and responsibility or his guilt and sinfulness.

In all historical confessions (symbols, creeds) *the forgiveness of sins* shows through as the fundamental reality in relations between God and man, between man and man. Faithful Christians do not live, in their personal lives or in their church communities, on ideas, or dogmatic formulations, or on ethical norms. All this can be, and is indispensable for the continuity of the Church of the present with that of the apostles. But the real meaning of life is the awareness that we live on the basis of the forgiveness of sins, granted as a gift of the sovereign grace of God. We can find no just relationship with the people around us if we do not realize that we need the forgiveness of others and that we are called to forgive. Theology fails to reach its true depths if it does not grasp this ultimate truth in all its historical and literary, dogmatic and liturgical studies. What is involved is a mystery—in the genuine sense of the word—free of any mythical or irrational speculations. It is a mystery in the sense that no scientific or philosophical category is sufficient to explain this relationship, and that the same is true of the most profound psychological or sociological studies. Whoever thinks that it is possible to—and that he can—explain the ultimate realities of sin and forgiveness by means of reason, ethics, or psychology, remains far from what is decisive in human life, from what is the real dynamic in the relationship between man and God, between man and his neighbour. The understanding of other men goes well beyond the mere level of social—or even the most noble-minded ethical—conventions.

From this we can also understand why theology and confessions of faith have so long talked of the Creator Spirit (*Creator Spiritus*). By this they did not mean some sort of mystical influence which miraculously intervenes in our lives. What they really meant to say was that truly to understand man, to understand his existential relationship to God and to other men, a much more profound and penetrating method is needed than that of science with its reason, ethical conventions with their norms, its clever intuitions, or its careful studies of natural and psychological processes. It is on this deep level that we encounter what we call 'love' or 'joyful hope'—that which does not surrender even at times of the worst failure or of unavoidable misfortune.

The ground of hope

This is the ground on which our most intensive spiritual struggles and dialogues have been and will be undertaken. We are not going to discuss the right of rational criticism, of scientific precision, of technical progress or even the necessity of social revolutions, both economic and political. We are in the midst of a world-wide revolution which extends to every region of personal and social life. We may even agree with Marxists that today's world-wide tensions in fact spring from the hidden class struggle which one finds in every country in the world. But our dialogues are not just with Marxists. We see before us endless ranks of modern sceptics and atheists (often in anti-communist guises, because there are many atheists among anti-communists), and we encounter writers and philosophers who are themselves completely disoriented and who seek to describe the situation from which there is no escape, the impasse in which modern man finds himself. Then there are the existentialists who have turned away from the objective world to discover in the depths of the human personality that man, like a swimmer in a stormy sea without a compass, must live out his own life, deprived of any kind of certainty or of any meaning in his own existence. And we have before us the countless multitude of those who accept life only to enjoy it and lose themselves in their sometimes petty, sometimes significant anxieties.

It seems to me that in the midst of all this, our dialogue with committed Marxists is relatively the most hopeful. I do not know if we Christians are properly equipped for this mission. But the Gospel gives the most real insight into the very depths of human life and the most comprehensive understanding of society and history, and especially of the future. The Gospel unites us with the first witnesses of the Old Testament and with the sufferings of the present moment, but it directs our thinking ever towards the future. The Church is not a static institution bound to the established order and furnished with the sure means of salvation. The Church is a community of believers always on the move, who radiate an atmosphere of humility towards the God of holiness and mercy. The Church is ever mindful of man, in all his strengths and weaknesses, in his joys and despairs. All this helps us to believe that he who leads us defenceless to the shadow of his cross, is and will be the final victor.

THE CHRISTIAN PEACE CONFERENCE

Freedom and flexibility

Our Christian Peace Conference can only be understood fully on the basis of what I have just said. It did not grow up as a mere political organization concerned with peace, one which, under the banner of Christianity, would pursue certain political goals. It emerged from the tensions of the post-war world, in particular under the influence of the intensification of the cold war. Its purpose has been to awaken Christians to their responsibility to do everything in their power to prevent another world-wide catastrophe. It was the subject of much suspicion and criticism—both theological and political—from several sides. We are much indebted to our colleagues from many churches, countries and continents, but it is we ourselves who must give an account of the goals and meaning of our work. We may reply to those critical voices: the Christian Peace Conference (CPC) has been working for ten years; it has grown and is still growing; it has a life of its own and thus gives an answer to the question whether it is needed, and why it exists. But we do not just want to take cover in the face of attacks, criticisms and doubts. We must constantly examine ourselves and think about the place and meaning of our activity. But I shall say at least a few words by way of a personal answer.

We are a movement, and in no way a group of official representations of various ecclesiastical institutions. We gratefully welcomed the co-operation of those churches who from the outset in 1958 joined our movement and undertook to share the responsibility for our activity. And we are glad whenever this or that church applies for admission or at least sends a delegate or observer. Churches as established or traditional institutions have their place among us, and the so-called 'Peace Churches' (for example, the Mennonites, the Church of the Brethren, or the Quakers) have supported us from the beginning. But even so, our work is not founded on an official union of churches. We are still open to groups and individuals who wish to work with us on their own, rather than their church's responsibility. In this way, our activity gains in freedom and flexibility. It is important that official representatives of the historic or of the 'peace' churches should be prepared to listen to the voice of groups and individuals, to take seriously what they have to say, and to consider their opinions as responsible and as valid as their own. We would wish to remain on this basis, although we are glad to accept the hand stretched out to us by the organized churches.

We believe that this character of the CPC is an important reminder to the historic churches that the Church of Christ is not exclusive and that it can adapt itself to the urgent tasks of the present time. The real Church is always being born anew, always in tension with tradition and its official labels. We in no way wish to devalue the ecumenical bodies seeking the union of the organized churches. Not only are we happy to work with those who are prepared to extend us a hand, but we gratefully welcome their suggestions. At the same time, however, we have decided to remain a movement which has its own organization and rules, one that is, to be sure, ever in danger of becoming institutionalized, but whose real mission is to remain open to all, and to be ready both to absorb new collaborators from every side and to change its structure according to the needs of the given moment. I would not wish to claim that we have achieved this flexibility, but I believe that this must be the characteristic basis of our movement.

A stronger basis

But something else, something more important is also involved. We began our activity in the context of a particular historical situation. The cold war is dying out but has left behind permanent traces in the relations not only among nations, but also among churches. We have been accused of defending a certain conception of East European government. This was an unjust rebuke. But it is true that we have tried to interpret and defend that which the East as well as certain parts of the 'Third World' have contributed to the process of history, and which must be taken into account in the struggle for the future peaceful organization of the world. I am not referring to the official politics of the East European governments, but to that which has emerged as a result of the catastrophe of 1939–45, and which has been a historical corrective to the whole structure of Western society. I can remember from my own ecumenical experience how, for a certain time, the words 'peace' or 'peaceful coexistence' were looked on with distrust, as if they had been hung out as signboards by the countries of East Europe. The principle of the 'open society' was proclaimed, as it were, against socialist society, and the Western forms of civil liberty were regarded as the permanent norm of world order.

The roots of the World Council of Churches and confessional ecumenical bodies go back to pre-war times; ours lie in the period when, in the ruins of the post-war world, it was necessary to seek stronger bases for peaceful coexistence than those offered by Western, so-called bourgeois or liberal democracy. We bear the mark of the historical situation in which we were born, even though we must be always open towards the new, and towards the changes in the march of history.

An ear to the ground

We are in the midst of a fearful struggle between rich and poor, between the holders of economic power and financial control on the one hand, and, on the other, groups which are fighting not just for political forms of civil freedom, but also for higher standards of living, for social equality, and for guarantees against the arrogance and exploitation of the rich.

It is possible to say, with a certain circumspection, that the significance of the situation of the world today lies in a vast class struggle. We are not thinking here in terms of Marxist formulations, although from them we can learn much about the historical process especially over the last fifty years. In mentioning the class struggle, however, we do not mean a struggle between the working and the owning classes, but rather that all the nations of human society now find themselves in a struggle to prevent the decisions about the future from being taken just by the large, rich nations. Millions of people are struggling for guarantees against hunger and political impotence, against ignorance and a growing death rate. We do not wish here to use cheap clichés. But we constantly remind ourselves and the community of Christians that underlying today's restiveness and the crises in Europe, Asia, Africa and America is an attempt by the holders (often anonymous) of wealth and political power to halt the revolutionary or peaceful struggle against the unscrupulous selfishness of rich classes and nations. Our peaceful struggle does not seek to create just a peaceful community of the powerful. On the contrary, its concern is to think deeply about the preconditions for a genuine and lasting peace. And lasting peace, I would repeat, is unthinkable so long as affluent and overfed peoples stand on one side, while on the other stand the hungry and poor.

This is also the sense of our understanding of revolution. We are not formulating a theology of revolution, but we are seeking a theology deeply rooted in the mystery of the Gospel and thereby open towards the struggles of poor peoples and nations, even if this sometimes must come to armed conflict. At the moment we are giving careful attention to the intellectual movement among young people, especially the students in universities and colleges. At the same time, we ask ourselves whether the working class, in the rich countries, has not come to the end of its creative role in political and social struggle and whether the banner of political and social progress has not passed into the hands of the awakening young intelligentsia. In all our planning and activity we put our ear to the ground and try to estimate where the real *avant-garde* of today's humanity is standing—and fighting. Without the working class it cannot win, but there are times when labour must be aroused from inaction and lethargy.

The purpose of these remarks is to explain the meaning of our movement within the context of ecumenical activity, but also within that of the contemporary crisis of mankind and the present danger of war. We are called upon to speak out, in all openness, so that we can see the universal significance of our own personal calling, a universality which transcends the limitations of contemporary church forms and political power *blocs*. Only when we penetrate to the very core of the actual responsibilities the present situation imposes on those who profess and call themselves Christian, when we come face to face with what is actually taking place now, will we find genuine freedom and conviction.

HISTORY, FAITH, POLITICS

What do we mean by historical orientation in the struggle of faith and in political decision-making?

Every historical event and personality must be fully understood in the perspective of subsequent historical development. The passage of months and years sometimes lends significant importance to events that were hardly noticed at the time they occurred. How many thinkers and public servants are seen in their real significance and importance only decades later? We cannot even imagine how people we look up to with respect and devotion acquire, as time goes by, an almost mythical aura. It is probably not possible in any other way. Historical events and personalities have no way of influencing the present other than the way offered by our faith, confidence, love, devotion or disagreement, repugnance or hatred. If we think of such names as Jan Hus, Jan Amos Komensky, Karel Havlicek Frantisek Palacky, T. G. Masaryk, or Marx, Engels, or Lenin— we soon realize that these men live for us in forms characterized by respect and confidence, or by the existential hatred of their followers or enemies. The same is true of the dates of great historical upheavals, for example November 7, 1917, October 28, 1918, September 30, 1938, May 9, 1945, February 25, 1948, or, let us add, August 21, 1968. These dates mean something to us not just for what empirically happened on them, but because they reflect everything which preceded and followed them; they are the marks of our pleasures and hopes, or of our disappointments and personal or national tragedies. But I repeat, this is the only possible way. History is not just a procession of favourable events which can be ascertained and described from the memory of contemporary men or on the basis of written documents in archives. History is only history when events are constantly transformed in the minds, hopes, decisions and actions of individuals, nations or cultural and social units. What matters is the comprehension, the understanding, the agreement or criticism of the actions or desires of the generations which follow. I mention this so that it will be clear that whenever we talk about historical epochs or years, we are not just passive observers of that which has been; we do not accept historical events and personalities as fatefully determining our present beliefs, decisions, and goals. We struggle with every event and personality on the basis of our own responsibility. And we carry on their meaning and content as they were creatively transformed by our struggle, creative thought and by practical decisions.

THE CROSSROADS OF SOCIALISM

This is the light in which I would like the following observations about the outcome and meaning of the year 1968 to be viewed. It is not the date that is important. When 1968 began cannot be precisely determined; it had already begun in the preceding years. But it helps us if we at least try to see what that year means for us, and how it has affected even our theological thought and our hopes and fears in our personal and in the wider socio-political and cultural life.

How many times during the last few years have we felt that we were living in a watershed age or in a crisis of history; that we stood at the beginning of a period in which we could act on the basis of definite foresight and that we could anticipate in some measure the development of domestic and international situations? We mentioned in our explanation that after the first world war prominent thinkers and statesmen expected that thenceforth things would develop in an orderly way, without war or serious conflict. And we see that other statesmen and thinkers (let alone ordinary citizens) saw November 7, 1917, as a decisive moment in favour of a certain way of constructing human society, as a determining factor for the logic of the future. (In passing, however, we should also recall the myth of the thousand year Third Reich and of the definitive victory of the Nordic race over the rest of the world.) In such things we are much more critical today and feel in our bones, so to speak, the relativity of our historical ideas, conjectures and ideals. 1968 more or less brutally confronted us with the fact that we stand in the midst of a historical whirlwind, in which it is only with great difficulty that we can detect any sense or logic. There is danger that we may lose sight of the great struggle between rich and poor, the powerful and the weak, between the advanced societies and those nations which are only slowly fighting their way towards self-determination and some sort of minimal level of culture and development. But our calculations and appraisals of what may come and of where evolution is tending persistently crumble in our hands.

After the second world war we believed, with some reason, that a stable world order would be maintained by the two great powers which had acquired world leadership following the fall of Berlin and Rome and the exhaustion of London and Paris. Today we are witnesses of a serious crisis in human society, for neither one of these two powers, not even the two of them together, have been able to control the political and social, the economic and cultural, the moral and spiritual problems of mankind. If we add to this the enigma of the People's Republic of China and its designs and goals, the contemporary world takes on a gloomy aspect of uncertainty and unpredictability. The United States of America does not know what to do even over such a small country as Vietnam. It has shown that not even vast military power and unprecedented material wealth are any guarantee of wisdom in international affairs. These things have been used to bring political or economic pressure against small countries. The Presidential elections of 1968 revealed among the American people a political helplessness and ended in a way which shows penetratingly that if a creative political and social order is to be built, far more is needed than can be acquired by power, welfare and financial supremacy. To this we must add the uneasiness, the political and social tension in Latin America.

All the economic and political pressure of the powerful Northern nations has revealed itself in all its inauspicious sterility and practical ineffectiveness. The hundreds of thousands of dead in Indonesia, the growing number of military *coups d'etat* in Africa—such events are disquieting not just because they show us the complexity of national and political development in the 'Third World' countries, but even more because there we are witnesses to the disruption of international order. How simple international society seemed in the days when various European states were strong, with much of the rest of the world their colonial subjects. We know that the idea of the excellence of the old colonial system is nonsense. But we are aware of a deep conflict between what we consider historical, political and international progress, on the one hand, and our ethical or spiritual notions about free and human society on the other.

We are not concerned just with the Western world or with the storms and bloody sacrifices in the developing countries. We are also concerned with what is taking place in the socialist world, especially in connection with the events of 1968. At the beginning of the 1950s we believed that the partnership of the two great socialist powers—the Soviet Union and the People's Republic of China—would guarantee the victory of socialism not only in Europe and Asia, but gradually throughout the rest of the world as well. Today we are confronted by the question, I should almost say the enigma, of how to go about building world socialism in the face of such a deep contradiction between these two gigantic powers.

But the question of power, however important it may be, is only one of the very serious questions concerning socialist society. In one of my essays I have noted the danger that the emphasis on the dictatorship of the proletariat and on the inevitable role of violence in the building of socialism may dull the awareness of the leading representatives of this society to the special content of truly creative socialism, with its programme and goal of a free, deeply human, culturally fruitful society. Dictatorship and power are but forms and instruments of a particular, revolutionary moment. The time comes when it is necessary to transfer the centre of gravity of socialist construction to human commitment, to free decision-making, to better, purer relations of confidence and mutual understanding, and to an atmosphere of genuine freedom without economic pressure, without inequality, without exploitation, and without tutelage. If socialist society is too long maintained by the external authority of power, by the pressure of directives and commands from above, an internal weakening sets in and its resistance towards what we call bourgeois-capitalist society, declines. That which for a certain historical period is a guarantee of socialist society, can outlive its usefulness and create an atmosphere of laziness, cynicism and apathy; and it can even stifle the true consequences of socialism, joy in work and real solidarity among people.

Difficulties arise in the realm of socialism through the fact that individual nations do not remain, either historically or culturally, in the same situation. This does not mean that we have to measure the quality of their lives. But the variety of historical situations makes necessary different methods in political and social as well as in cultural and spiritual work. It is desirable that the statesmen and responsible builders of socialist society should have a good sociological and psychological understanding of the differences in atmosphere of this or that country. There can be common goals despite socio-political differences in methods and emphases. But it can happen that in some countries socialism is stronger, more resilient, and more secure *vis à vis* external threats, the more there is within it the freedom to make decisions, and open criticism from above and below, and the less it is subject to external pressures and the influence of power politics. This is the meaning of what we call the humanization of socialist society.

One serious question that will be with us in both the near and distant future is how to preserve genuine community and effective co-operation among the socialist countries despite all historical and cultural differences. We know from recent experience that power politics and military methods can deprive socialist goals and the authority of those trying to build socialism, of their attractiveness for and influence on the most open and progressive elements in non-socialist societies. Ethically, historically, politically and even economically the future of socialist construction demands that the centre of gravity of all efforts be transferred from the area of power and external authority to that of the struggle for man in his whole, deeper condition. To repeat what was mentioned above, every society, including socialist society, can hold its own ground and win only if it is built on free commitment, on confidence among people, especially between the political leaders and the ordinary citizens, on responsibility for and pleasure in work, on courage and initiative in all kinds of work, and on a hopeful view of the future. People can put up for years with pressure, orders from outside authorities, and coercion, but there comes a time when they rise up against everything which does not convince them of the value, sense, and goals of the existing social order. Only then is it possible to expect an understanding among advanced, intelligent and responsible strata in the various areas of society, if socialism is to become a genuine guarantee of a higher—and not just politically higher—freedom, of an internal solidarity among people and a deeper culture of hearts and minds. Of course everything depends on the citizens of a socialist society being deeply aware of the bases of socialist freedom and humanism. Only thus can it be ensured that they will not flirt with freedom without responsibility and obligation, with the freedom of arbitrary selfishness.

We are confronted here with one of the most serious tasks of history. To build a society on the basis of personal advantage, free enterprise and profit is quite easy. We see from the history of the last two hundred years how thinkers, statesmen and educators have had, and still have, much work to do in protecting bourgeois society from the temptations of selfishness, greed, ethical anarchy and shameless money-seeking. It is also necessary to consider seriously the criticism of those who are opposed to the bourgeois society that the open and anonymous power of money can cleverly and quite honestly blind the democracy of these countries to ruthless exploitation and politico-economic domination over weaker countries. But we also hear the uneasiness in the conscience and understanding of those who realize all these dangers, and who struggle to renew the ideals of humanism, ideals which led to the revolt against feudalism and for which freedom was the precondition for the unfolding of all the deeper longings of real humanity. If today we talk about peaceful coexistence among nations, we are not thinking just about the mechanics of external coexistence, which, in the end, can be maintained only by some sort of agreement between the great powers. In the situation in which the human race finds itself today, we cannot underestimate the importance of such agreement, if we are to make at least some progress against the weapons of collective annihilation. But in the long run peace cannot be preserved if it is going to rely only on the deterrent strength of the nuclear weapons in the hands of the rival powers. The military and economic predominance of the great powers cannot long provide genuine international security. The dangers of their arrogance and their claim to the right to decide what is and is not correct or just, what is the truth and what a lie, have been and remain incalculable. We are entering a historical period wherein it will be necessary to unite all the creative influences of humanity, free responsibility and genuine solidarity in the service of brotherhood, so that we can lay the foundations of true peaceful coexistence in the deeper dimensions of man's personal and social life. Of course, related to this, is the question of whether the affluent, developed countries are ready to guarantee human dignity for the millions who are poor and hungry, suffering and oppressed.

The Dynamics of the Foundations

And here we raise the question of whether we, as so-called Christians, and our church institutions, are prepared for today's challenges and historical tasks. I shall not repeat what I said above about the lack of preparedness of certain individual Christians and churches in the decisive moments of history. The difficulty surely lies in the rapid flow, in the revolutionary events in the world today. Not even those of us who think that they understand the historical changes of the last fifty years, can be familiar with the ever growing complexities of international life, or even of that of their own nations. What we need is to immerse ourselves in the Gospel of the Old and New Testaments.

It may be that the shortcomings of today's families of Christian churches are rooted in the fact that we have not penetrated to the depth of the Gospel message of the presence of the God of Jesus of Nazareth in the abysses of human guilt and sin, impotence and death, dreams and hopes. There are signs that even in the great Christian formations something is going on that has to do with the very foundations of the Gospel and the Church. The Roman Catholic Church is today in spiritual turmoil and ethical and social uneasiness. In traditionally static countries, in so far as church fellowship is concerned, protests are developing against the apathy of the Church and against the ecclesiastical injustices of priests and bishops, while in traditionally Catholic countries the Church is ceasing to be a supporter of the rich and the powerful. It is looking for a new content of liturgical and sacramental life, or, perhaps better put, it is digging to the foundations of what was, in the apostolic Church, liturgical and sacramental community. Desire for the free fulness of the faith in the victorious Christ risen from the dead is awakening even in the Orthodox Church. Surely we Protestants must not lag behind in desire for new wonders and gifts from the Holy Spirit.

Today, even in the socialist countries, the time arrives when thinkers and builders of the new order begin to listen to the living witnesses of the Gospel, and to seek their help in the struggle for a fuller, deeper, more creative human society. Genuine biblical faith has nothing in common with intellectual backwardness or social or political reaction. Shall we be able— in human terms—to open the sluice-gates of a genuinely prophetic and apostolic dynamic—a genuinely prophetic and apostolic revolutionary consciousness? Since January 1968 we had no right to say that we could not carry out our activities. And August 21 confirmed not only our solidarity with those nations which are fighting, but also opened new possibilities for us so that by our witness we might intensify the struggle for genuine freedom, humanity and unity.

We have no illusions that this job will be easy. We are aware of our weaknesses, of the lack of serious faith and of serious service in love. And we are aware of the many disturbing phenomena in our wider community. But these are precisely the reasons why we need a Gospel in its depths and breadth, so that we can stand firm and open our hearts to the members of our congregations, and to all who live around us, whether far or near, whether we are united with them in faith or separated from them by their unbelief. The struggle for a genuine humanity, in its dignity and freedom, in its weakness but also its creative capabilities, is for us not only a difficult task, but a joyous privilege as well, for today and for the future. We must approach this struggle as much with repentant humility as with courage and fortitude.

THE CONSOLATION OF THEOLOGY

When I began my life's work, I had no intention of following an academic course or of undertaking systematic scientific activity. After a certain amount of hesitation I entered with genuine pleasure into the work of a pastor and preacher. The changes which occurred during 1918 suddenly landed me at the Hus Theological Faculty in Prague. I was aware of my spiritual and theological shortcomings, and therefore set out to examine what was (as I have called it here) the classical line of Christianity from the time of the apostles onward. It was my way of coming to terms—albeit indirectly—with the shortcomings of modern theology, with the superficial anti-Catholic mood of the period, and with the fear of our average Christians vis à vis the socialist revolution which was approaching us from the East. During the crisis period of the 1930s I critically reviewed Masaryk's theological philosophy of religion, but when we came to be threatened by the barbarian danger of Nazi Germany, I worked with Emmanuel Radl and several others to awaken an understanding of the deep roots of the humanistic democracy which Masaryk represented for us. After the signing of the Munich Agreement in 1938 we fell, and I transferred my own theological and publishing activity to the United States.

After the second world war and our return to Czechoslovakia a new struggle began, this one over the place of the Christian Church in a socialist society. This was a struggle on two fronts: on the one hand against the lack of understanding of a large number of Christians for historical phenomena and, on the other, against the prejudice with which the Church and theology were looked upon by the builders of the new order. In ecumenical circles we encountered not only prejudice but often open antipathy on the part of some of the representatives of the Western churches. Our work was burdened by many weaknesses, internal and tactical, but it could only be undertaken with the means available to us. Of course the biblical story of the unworthy servants applies to us. Our consolation is that the Lord God sustains even those who are in many ways not worthy of it, but who in certain situations find themselves placed in responsible positions. I believe this struggle has put our theology to a stringent test. Insufficiencies of depth and purity were often revealed; but I can say that this very struggle, within the Church and in public, has served to deepen and refine it.

My Christological view of the Old Testament, of the Early Church and of the history of Christianity has made me sure of the fact that there is, outside the Christian faith, no intellectually more penetrating view of history, society and man. And the deeper a man descends towards the centre of the apostolic message of the Cross and the Resurrection, the better he understands the meaning of the life of Jesus, and thus the more courageously he can devote himself to today's personal, social and political sufferings and tasks.

In closing, I confess that theology has always been to me the true joy and that if I had to decide today, I should again choose it as my life's work.

Bibliography

Bibliography of the most important works of Josef Hromadka. Roman numerals refer to the chapter to which the individual works are related. All works are in Czech except those marked with an asterisk, which are in English.

II

Christianity and Scientific Thought (1922)
The Central Principles of Protestantism (1925)
Catholicism and the Struggle for Christianity (1925)
The Ways of a Protestant Theologian (1927)
Palacky and his Significance for the Czech National Revival (1926)
Principles of the Evangelical Church of Czech Brethren (1927)
Masaryk (1930)
Masaryk and Dostoevsky (1931)
Christianity in Thought and Life (1931)
Luther (1935)
Calvin (1936)
The Meaning of the Czech Brethren Reformation (1939)

III

Don Quixote of the Czech Philosophy (1939)
*Doom and Resurrection (1945) (German title: Sprung über die Mauer, 1961)

IV

The New Czechoslovakia (1946)

Between East and West (1946)

Communism and Christianity (1946)

Theology and the Church (1949)

Four Confessions (1951)

From the Reformation to Tomorrow (1956)

*Theology between Yesterday and Tomorrow (1957) (German title: Theologie und Kirche zwischen Gestern und Morgen, 1960)

Gospel on the Way to Man (1958) (German, 1961)

*A Gospel for Atheists (1958)

On the Threshold of Dialogue (1963) (German, 1964) (partly translated into English; published in Communio Viatorum, 1964, p. 119ff. published in Prague)

and several shorter works, particularly articles in various journals.